IT'S A BOY

WOMEN WRITERS
ON RAISING SONS

EDITED BY ANDREA J. BUCHANAN

SEAL PRESS

IT'S A BOY:
WOMEN WRITERS ON RAISING SONS

Jennifer Lauck's "It Takes a Village" was previously published in different form and is reprinted with permission of Atria Books, an imprint of Simon & Schuster Adult Publishing Group, from *Show Me the Way: A Memoir in Stories* by Jennifer Lauck. Copyright © 2004 by Jennifer Lauck.

Marion Winik's "Our Bodies, Their Selves" is reprinted from *The Lunchbox Chronicles: Notes from the Parenting Underground* by Marion Winik, copyright © 1998 by Marion Winik. Used by permission of Pantheon Books, a division of Random House, Inc.

Published by
Seal Press
1400 65th Street, Suite 250
Emeryville, CA 94608

9 8 7 6 5

Library of Congress Cataloging-in-Publication Data

It's a boy : women writers on raising sons / edited by Andrea J. Buchanan.
   p. cm.
ISBN-10: 1-58005-145-6
ISBN-13: 978-1-58005-145-3

1. Boys. 2. Mothers and sons. 3. Parenting. I. Buchanan, Andrea J.
HQ775.I77 2005
306.874'3'0973—dc22
2005014839

Cover design by Gia Giasullo, studio eg
Interior design by Domini Dragoone
Printed in the United States of America by Berryville
Distributed by Publishers Group West

To Nate,
my sweet boy.

CONTENTS

WILL BOYS BE BOYS?

THE VELVET UNDERGROUND

SHAPE-SHIFTER

Introduction

The most popular question any pregnant woman is asked—aside from "When are you due?"—has got to be, "Are you having a girl or a boy?" When I was pregnant with my daughter over six years ago, I was new to maternity, so it took me a while to recognize that all of my conversations with strangers would inevitably follow a similar script:

"When are you due?"

"June."

"Do you know what you're having?"

"Yes."

"A boy or a girl?"

"A girl."

And then the strangers would either rhapsodize about cute little girl babies in pink or tell me I had no idea what I was in for. On my way to being a mother for the first time, I had to agree with that sentiment in its most general interpretation.

The second time I was pregnant, I barely had room in my brain to remember I was pregnant. I was busy raising a preschooler, writing a book, working as an editor, running a household. When strangers asked me when I was due, it would take a moment to register with me what, in fact, they were talking about. Then I would look down and see my enormous stomach and remember: *Oh, yes, the baby.* This time I knew where that first question would be leading, so I would spill all without coercion. "October. A boy—second baby," I'd blurt, anticipating the arc of the conversation and hoping to have effectively ended it.

But I was wrong. The news that I was having a boy was tantalizing to these strangers, these street philosophers primed to offer advice on parenting to a pregnant woman. "A boy!" they'd say. "You must be so happy!" As though I wouldn't be if I were carrying a girl. Or, "A boy! Your husband must be proud!" As if he'd be disappointed to have a daughter. Countless people told me how easy boys are, how loving, how sweet, how special, how different from girls.

It surprised me.

Becoming a mother to a daughter had felt natural to me—after all, I am a daughter, I have a mother, I feel I have a small amount of insight into the relationship. And I grew up with sisters. Girls and women, I thought, were things I could understand. Becoming a mother to a son felt strange, even a little unnatural, and I was unnerved by the happiness of strangers who celebrated my boy-to-be in a way I couldn't comprehend.

Talking about my boy apprehension proved to be a sensitive topic: Before I became pregnant with my son, Nate, I had confessed to a friend that I didn't ever want to have a boy, that I was afraid of having a son. I told her that if I was ever going to have another baby, I'd want to be certain it was a girl, and I joked that now that I'd said that out loud, I'd be doomed to have a son for sure. My friend, the mother of a son, took this personally: We did not speak for three months. Once I was pregnant with Nate and eager to hash out the differences between boys and girls, other mothers of sons seemed to miss the point of my questions: "But boys *are* easier!" one friend told me. "I don't understand," said another. "Girls are more work. Why would you not want to have a son?" It was hard to get past these kinds of preconceived notions, plus the ones I was battling myself, and get the honest truth about boyness, if there even was one.

After Nate was born and I had fully and happily surrendered to the world of boy, my ambivalence reconciled, I began working on an essay about boyness. Usually I write at lightning speed, but this piece dragged on and on, taking not the usual hour to spill onto my computer screen, but days, weeks, months. Each time I returned to it, I felt resistant, blocked. There was so much to say—too much to say. What was I trying to confront in the piece? What was I really trying to get at? What was the point?

As I investigated this, I spoke and exchanged emails with other mothers and writers about mothering boys and girls, and I asked the following questions: Are there differences between mothering a son and mothering a daughter? Are the ideas we have about boys and girls based on real differences between them, or do our ideas about their differences inform their behavior? Do boys truly love their mothers differently? Are girls really "difficult"? Are boys really "easy"? Do these stereotypes about boy and girl babies change in toddlerhood? Adolescence?

The conversation this sparked inspired me not only to finish my piece on being the reluctant mother of a boy, but also to embark on two essay collections about mothering boys and mothering girls—not instructional tomes or guidebooks, but literary explorations of what it means to mother sons and daughters, and the differences between girls and boys. This book, It's a Boy, and its companion piece, It's a Girl, due out in 2006, are the result.

The essays in It's a Boy are grouped in four sections: "It's a Boy," which features tales of ambivalence, love, and newborn babies; "Will Boys Be Boys?," which explores bullying, violence, and redemption, the otherness and the potential of boys; "The Velvet Underground," which examines gender roles and what we expect from our sons; and "Shapeshifter," which tackles the ever-changing nature of boyness and a mother's role as her son grows.

By far the topic on which I received the most submissions was what I ended up calling "prenatal boy apprehension": stories of mothers who either were conflicted about having sons or had never considered the possibility of having anything other than a daughter. Eight of these essays exploring the mystery of baby boys comprise the first section, "It's a Boy." My own essay, "It's a Boy!" focuses on my experience of wanting a second girl—and my fears that what those happy strangers told me might come true: that I might love a son more. Jody Mace ("You've Got Male!") and Stephany Aulenback ("Expectations") ponder similar concerns as Mace wonders if she can even relate to a Power Ranger–loving boy and Aulenback attempts to trace her boy reluctance back to her parents. Novelist Caroline Leavitt ("A Son's Love") is surprised by the unexpected sweetness and intensity of the love she feels for her son, and Ona Gritz ("Son of a Guy") explains what it's like to love a boy with a temperament so different from her own—and so much like her ex-husband's. Marrit Ingman feels out of her element in "Exile in Boyville," and Jennifer Margulis ("My Three Sons") and Marjorie Osterhout ("Breaking the Curse") both come to terms with different kinds of family legacies around having boys.

In the second section, "Will Boys Be Boys?" writers further explore the notion of the "otherness" of boys, including violence, preschool bullies, "boy" literature, the freedom and power of boyhood, and dreams of a boy that never was. Karen E. Bender reveals what it's like to be blacklisted as the mother of a pint-sized biter in "The Bully's Mother," and Jennifer Lauck shares a story about her son, a group of boys, and knives in "It Takes a Village." Rochelle Shapiro ("Will Boys Be Boys?") contrasts her experience of having a son with the theoretical ideal she had in mind as a consciousness-raising feminist of the 1970s. Gayle Brandeis learns to reconcile her pacifism with her son's desire to learn archery and play paintball in "Zen and the Art of Extracurricular Activities," and Kate Staples ("Reading to My Son") wonders if she can ever impart the kind of girlish love she had for literature to a little boy who prefers chewing books to reading them. Robin Bradford watches her eight-year-old son with friends and reflects on how mothering a son has opened her up to the world of boys in "Becoming a Boy"; Faulkner Fox ("Full House") contemplates the girls she never had while she learns to throw a baseball with her two sons; and, in one of the book's most poignant essays, Susan Ito ("Samuel") wonders what life would have been like with the son she never had.

In "The Velvet Underground," we find writers exploring gender expectations, both cultural and personal, as they navigate the distance between mother and son. Gwendolen Gross ("Entering the Den of Math") writes of feeling a pang of separation from her son as he takes a stereotypical boy's delight in numbers over words. Suzanne Kamata ("Chonan") and Katie Kaput ("Things You Can't Teach") face intimidating cultural expectations about their sons, as Kamata raises a prized "oldest son" in Japan and Kaput, a transsexual girl, struggles to parent a boy. Susan O'Doherty ("The Velvet Underground") grapples with her family history around what boys are made of and tries to find a way to nurture her son's softer side even as she recognizes his need for protection. Jodi Picoult ("Scaredy-Cat") and Catherine Newman ("Pretty Baby") write about their sons' divergence from the cultural norm that dictates a boy should be brave and not interested in watching, let alone acting out, performances of *The Nutcracker*. And Marion Winik ("Our Bodies, Their Selves") realizes her boys are no longer young enough to be innocent of her body now that they are coming into their own.

Finally, "Shapeshifter" considers the changing role of mothers as boys grow. These tales of adapting mothers and evolving sons mostly concern teenage boys, but Jamie Pearson tackles the topic of a mother's first decision about her son's body—to circumcise or not—in "Making the Cut." Maura Rhodes ("[Almost] All Grown Up") and Katie Allison Granju ("The Teenage Boy") write about how their mothering changes as their sons morph into men, and Jacquelyn Mitchard muses on her son's quiet rite of passage into manhood in "The Day He Was Taller." Melanie Lynne Hauser's "Shapeshifter" chronicles the teenage boy's toddlerlike, lightning-quick shift between demanding grown-up independence and wanting maternal comfort—from the viewpoint of the mother who must watch it all and remain constant, unchanging. Lisa Peet contrasts her unpleasant memories of high school boys with the teenage boy she lives with now ("Space Invader"), and Kathryn Black ("Surrounded by Children") writes about how her two sons have transformed her from a mother of two to a mother of many children.

In January 2005, as I was working on compiling this book, the president of Harvard, Larry Summers, gave a speech he would find hard to live down in the coming months. Speaking at an academic conference to an audience of scientists and engineers, he posited that "innate differences" between men and women might explain why women are underrepresented in the sciences. Not sexism, nor bias toward people who bear children, nor even the cultural consensus that women are worse than men in math and science: The defining fact that is keeping women from reaching the upper levels of the scientific professions was, in his mind, "aptitude," which he directly tied to gender.

A month later, a study published in the journal *Behavioral Neuroscience* found that while there was a slight "gender gap" between male and female rhesus monkeys in performing certain tasks involving spatial memory, these gaps disappeared when female monkeys were given training appropriate for the tasks on which they were being tested. The researcher said, "It is important to note that in the rhesus monkey, we only find the sex difference in spatial memory, not other cognitive domains." She went on to conclude, "A lot of times researchers will just interpret any kind of sex difference as evidence for a rigid, biological difference. This study really does tend to argue that the difference is biologically set, perhaps, but that it's also really easy to change if you work on it."

In March, just a month later, researchers who sequenced the human X chromosome discovered that females are genetically more varied than males. "It turns out 15% of genes [in females' second X-chromosome] escape inactivation altogether, each of which now becomes a candidate for explaining differences between men and women," said Robin Lovell-Badge, of the National Institute for Medical Research, U.K. "Moreover, another 10% are sometimes inactivated and sometimes not, giving a mechanism to make women much more genetically variable than men." Reports of this discovery found it hard to resist gendered language, as evidenced in the purple prose of the *Washington Post*, which breathlessly announced, "She was slow to reveal her secrets, but the X chromosome has now bared it all."

It seems surprising to me that even now, in the twenty-first century, we are still divided between science and anecdote when it comes to our basic assumptions about gender. In his speech, Summers mentioned his own toddler daughters as an example of how, even as young girls, females seem to be instinctively nurturing, saying, "I guess my experience with my two and a half year old twin daughters who were not given dolls and who were given trucks, and found themselves saying to each other, look, daddy truck is carrying the baby truck, tells me something." On the surface, this story seems to confirm gender expectations—proof that even given "boy" toys like trucks, girls revert to the kind of nurturing play typical of females. But I could counter this with an anecdote that subverts gender expectations: A few weeks ago, over breakfast in a restaurant, my two-and-a-half-year-old son Nate took one of his toy cars, put it underneath his shirt, and cradled it on his belly, saying, "Oh, my baby!"

What can we conclude from this?

I think the safest thing we can conclude is that our expectations are flawed, and that extrapolating theories about gender from isolated facts or even anecdotes is risky, at best. All questions of whether men and women are from wildly disparate planets aside, the range of what is "boy behavior" and what is "girl behavior" seems to be fluid, flexible, and highly specific to personal experience. The stories of the mothers and sons in this book are reflective of that. They are personal and specific, dynamic and multifaceted, and grounded in the day-to-day experience of living with boys—some of whom play "car crash" with trucks and some of whom turn trucks into babies; all of whom deserve to experience the full range of human emotion, which knows no gender.

ANDREA J. BUCHANAN
May 2005
Philadelphia, Pennsylvania

IT'S
A BOY

Expectations

STEPHANY
AULENBACK

Long before I got pregnant, I began to fantasize about my imaginary daughter. I rarely imagined having a son. So a few weeks ago, when the ultrasound technician's pointer indicated my unborn son's own rather obvious pointer, I was as shocked as I have ever been in my life.

Although the rational part of me knew that statistically there was pretty much a 50 percent chance of having a baby of either sex, the superstitious part of me believed that, while baby girls were of course born naturally of their mothers, baby boys required work. In the tradition of old wives' tales, you had to do something difficult and deliberate to conceive them—it involved an esoteric kind of meditation, maybe, or an unusual physical technique, perhaps, or both. Obviously, female had to be the "default" sex. Look at Henry VIII. Look at all those millions of Chinese people, casting aside all those unwanted baby girls in the streets. Some part of me must have had the smug, secret notion that I would be cosmically rewarded for valuing what so many others on the planet had historically devalued. It seemed clear. Because I wanted a girl, I would get her.

My fixation on the sex of the baby was ridiculous, I knew. I'd had four miscarriages prior to this pregnancy; I should have been overjoyed and grateful to have finally achieved a healthy, viable pregnancy at all. And I was. Oh, I always was. At least, the logical, rational part of me always was. I have to admit, though, that for a few days after that ultrasound, I reeled.

In the car, on the way home from the fetal assessment clinic, I tried to explain—ostensibly to my husband—why I was so disappointed. "I feel like I'd know what to do with a girl," I told him. "I know how it feels to be a girl. I'd be able to help her through the tricky stuff. I don't know anything about boys and their tricky stuff."

"Oh, boys don't have any tricky stuff," said David, trying to be reassuring. He laughed. "They're really easy. Once they hit puberty, all they think about is sex. They don't care about anything else. And that's pretty much it, until they die."

I was not reassured.

Over the next few days, guiltily flailing around for another explanation for my distress over having a boy, I turned—in the time-honored way—to blaming my mother. On a number of occasions, my mother had told me that, while I'd never given her more than a moment's trouble, my little brother had been so demanding that if he'd been born first, he'd have been an only child. My mother was also fond of telling me about playground studies on sex differences in toddlers. "Little girls spend their time *talking* to each other about *relationships*," she'd told me on the phone. "Little boys *run around* making *weird noises*."

According to my mother, all men were difficult—but the men in my immediate family were *notoriously* difficult. Having had firsthand experience with those difficult men, I wholeheartedly agreed with her.

Perversely, though, I figured this was somehow my mother's fault. I had the vague notion that it had something to do with the way she'd handled them.

Although my mother was very open with me about how difficult my little brother had been to raise, I'd secretly continued to nurse a childhood grudge against her based on my belief that, in spite of how difficult he was—or maybe because of it—she'd always preferred him to me. Even today my childhood friends marvel over how he'd had her wrapped around his little finger—though, to be fair, he'd had almost everyone wrapped around his little finger. Where I was dough faced, obedient, and sullen, he was cherubic, mischievous, and charming—and that difference between us may explain the way my mom seemed to light up around him. Because when I tried to think of examples of times she had favored him over me specifically *because he was a boy*, I couldn't think of many. Sure, now and then she'd make me do the dishes while he was sent outside to play; she'd insisted that was because I was older, not because I was a girl. Sure, there was a time when she spent the two hours before bed reading and playing alone with him every evening. When I asked why we couldn't have a similar private time together, she explained he was a little behind in school and that I did so well because I'd already gotten four years alone with her before he'd been born. So, while there were signs like these, open to interpretation, I couldn't come to any definite conclusions.

Still, I remembered my little brother eternally getting into some kind of trouble and my mother fretting over it. When he was five or six, he disappeared repeatedly on his way home from kindergarten—distracted by other children, he'd stop to play with them and forget to come home. My mother and I would drive around our small town looking for him for hours. Mom would shout his name frantically out the open windows of the family car the entire time. Now and then, I'd join in and call out dutifully. When he was a young teen, he and a couple of friends went camping and accidentally started a raging forest fire. When he was sixteen or seventeen, he got kicked out of private school for having sex with his girlfriend on the stage in the auditorium. In his early twenties, he dropped out of college and refused to get a job. All of this made my mother sick with worry. I suppose I equated "sick with worry" with "love."

But while I could remember the permanent anxious expression on my mother's face, her migraine headaches and her constantly wringing hands, I couldn't remember my brother's being made to suffer any consequences for his actions. I also remembered his asking for things—asking to do things, asking to have things—and getting them. They were things I would never have asked for, because I had assumed the answer would be "no." Because I had felt the answer *should* be "no."

Was my little brother difficult, as my mother had always maintained, because he was a boy? Was he difficult, as I'd always secretly believed, because of the way my mother had handled him, because of the way I felt she'd spoiled and coddled him? Or was he difficult simply because . . . he was difficult? It was easy to assume that my little brother's behavior and preferential treatment were due to his maleness. The more I thought about it, though, the more I realized it was possible that it had as much to do with his own particular temperament as it did with his sex—or his environment.

With my own baby boy still curled safely inside my belly, all I could conclude was that if I happened to have a willful, headstrong son, I would certainly try to handle it differently than my mother had. I'd be firmer. I'd say "no." Just because he had a Y chromosome, it didn't necessarily follow that my son was destined to be difficult, too.

As tempting as it was to blame my mother for my boy-child dread, it seemed hardly fair for her to shoulder it all by herself. So I moved on—to blaming my father.

In his midthirties, my father had become born again in our dim living room, on his knees in front of a flickering television evangelist. Soon afterward, instead of finding an established church to join, he took up with a cultlike fundamentalist Christian group that met in another living room—the living room of a local farming family who seemed to have modeled themselves on the Amish. Although even I, at the age of ten or twelve, could see that the central, most powerful figure in the group was the farmer's wife, the sect subscribed to extremely sexist views, even more sexist than those already inculcated in my dad through his years of Catholic school in the 1950s. As a result, we were often treated to litanies, at the dining room table or during the interminable Bible studies my father made us sit through, on the subservient role of women.

According to my father, a woman had one role in life and one role only—to create a safe and comfortable home for her family, one in which she could look after her husband and raise her children. A man, on the other hand, was free to do whatever he wished in the world, as long as it in some way provided financially for his family. And so, in combination with his extreme religious zealotry, my father was also a bit of a Willy Loman figure. Constantly trying to figure out a way to get rich quick and support us in the style to which his God had made him accustomed, he moved haphazardly from Amway to ill-fated real estate deals to various questionable multilevel marketing schemes.

My dad was—and still is—tall and good-looking, fond of hearing himself talk. He could be outrageously charming, gregarious, and enthusiastic. Sometimes he was self-confident to the point of complete self-centeredness, even self-indulgence. At other times he was deeply insecure—to the point of complete self-centeredness and self-indulgence. He was also prone to sudden inexplicable spells of rage or depression, which were terrifying to us, as children, in their unpredictability. In short, my father was what some people would call "an interesting character"—while others might say he was "clinically insane." I love him dearly, but I belong to the latter group (and maybe in more ways than one, it occurs to me now). However, as I tried to trace my reluctance to give birth to a boy to my relationship with my father, I began to understand (and this may seem counterintuitive) that because I'd thought of my father as an aberration for quite some time—in no way is he your "normal," "average" guy—I couldn't honestly say that I'd come to many conclusions about the male sex in general based on his example. Yes, he'd made me aware of the sexist views many men hold about women. And yes, at times I'd privately countered those views by coming up with unflattering generalizations about the male sex in turn—men were inherently violent, men were inherently more selfish and less sensitive, men were fixated on sex—but my heart had never been in it.

With both my mom and my dad off the hook, at least to a certain extent, and my beliefs and fears about the "innately difficult" nature of males exposed to myself as unfair and sexist in their own right, it was time for a little self-examination. Just why had I been so invested in the idea of having a daughter in the first place? My very best friend, my husband, was a man. A really terrific, really smart, really talented, really loving, really *good* man. In fact, the one or two times I'd ever considered having a son, I'd fantasized about raising not a combination of our genetic material but David's exact clone, a child completely untainted by my own DNA. After all, David himself had turned out well. And I thought we knew enough about his strengths and weaknesses, about his successes and disappointments, that we could turn out a new, improved version—like a better laundry detergent, only human.

If that seems slightly insane and more than slightly controlling, well, that's because it is.

Once that realization hit, I realized this: My fantasies about my imaginary daughter were similarly, if not more, insane and controlling. I began to see that they were linked to an earlier fantasy of mine: the "doing it all over again" fantasy, which had started back when I was in high school. This fantasy involved being reborn as an infant, but with all the knowledge and experience I'd acquired up to that point. I was sure that, given such an opportunity, I could get my life "right" a second time through. Over the years, though, the more I entertained this fantasy, the more it began to take a slightly nightmarish turn. Trying—and failing bleakly—to imagine, for instance, how the new, improved me would handle a notorious fifth-grade bully any differently than the way I had already (i.e., by making myself the fifth-grade equivalent of invisible), I'd think, *Who am I kidding? I'll still be the same person, constructed out of exactly the same genetic material. What if I can't do any better than I've already done? Worse—what if I screw up even more?*

That's when I gave up the "doing it all over again" fantasy and, instead, began inventing my imaginary daughter. My fantasies about her were rooted in both hubris and self-loathing. While on some level I felt that my childhood potential, my own talents and abilities, had not been properly acknowledged and nurtured, on another I believed my failures were less about that and more about my own particular set of innate character flaws. So my fantasies weren't so much about the things we, as mother and daughter, would do together. They were more about my daughter herself, her beauty, her intelligence, and her talent. They were about her vast set of accomplishments, about her amazing, marvelous life. All I'd have to do would be to create a rich environment in which to nurture her. My role as her mother would simply be to recognize her undeniable brilliance in whatever form it might take. One of those innate character flaws I recognized in myself is laziness—and nurturing someone else's talent probably seemed as if it would require, on the surface anyway, a lot less effort than nurturing my own.

It doesn't take a PhD to see that my fantasies about my imaginary daughter weren't actually about my imaginary daughter at all. (Which is good. Because while my imaginary daughter has a PhD—several, in fact—I don't.) They were fantasies about the girlhood I wished I'd had and, beyond that, about the life I wish I could be leading as an adult.

Most parents want their children to be better than they were, to lead happier, more successful lives. And, in most cases, that desire is good and healthy. In other cases, like mine, I'd have to say it falls into the category of "breathtakingly selfish." That selfishness seems obvious to me now, but until the ultrasound that surprised me a couple of weeks ago, it wasn't. Thinking about how terrible a mother I might have been to a daughter, how overbearing, how needy, how invested; thinking of just how much of a twisted personal stake I might have taken in the events of her life . . . well, I can see now that the baby currently curled inside my belly may very well have saved himself a lot of misery simply by turning out to be a boy.

Of course, there's every chance that I'll be a terrible mother to a boy, as well. But at least now I'm aware that I've got . . . issues, and that there are probably a lot more of them buried in the bottom of my personal baggage. At this point, I can only cross my fingers and hope that this baby continues to be, even when up against his crazy mother's most fervent wishes and most cherished expectations, very much *himself*.

It's a Boy!

ANDREA J.
BUCHANAN

I am thirty-eight weeks pregnant. It is ninety-eight degrees out, claustrophobically hot, and I am sweating as I cajole my three-year-old daughter up the steps to the building where my OB's office is.

"I don't *wanna* go in there!" she yells, cranky and fresh off a truncated playdate with her best friend. "I wanna go to *Zach's* house and play wif *Zach!*"

"Sorry, Sweetie," I tell her as matter-of-factly as possible while I hoist her and the stroller up the stairs. "I have to go to the doctor right now. We can play with Zach tomorrow. Hey, maybe the doctor will let you measure my belly!"

"I don't *want* to!" Scowl face.

"Maybe they'll have lollipops this time!"

"I don't *want* to!" Even scowlier face.

But I wrestle open the doors and thrust her through anyway. She wails and thrashes in her stroller as though I have pushed her into oncoming traffic. Her cries seem to fill up all available space in the hallway. This is by now a weekly occurrence.

21

By the time we get to the elevators, her hysterical sobs have given way to words. "Idon'twantto! Idon'twantto! Idon'twantto!" is her mantra as we wait for the doors to open. People around us are starting to stare. I stand calmly, as if it's perfectly routine to be subjecting my child to the unspeakable torture of having to be with me.

Some nurses who work on another floor in the building stand next to us, waiting for the elevator. They survey the scene, take in my enormous belly, my hyperventilating daughter.

"What are you having?" one of them asks me, speaking loudly over my daughter's cries and gesturing toward my belly.

"A boy," I tell her. She smiles. I know what's coming next.

"Oh, boys are wonderful," she says. "Boys are so much better than girls. You won't get tantrums like this with a boy, that's for sure."

At nine months pregnant, I've had nearly four months of engaging in very similar versions of this scene to prepare me for today's exchange. But I am never fully prepared. Even knowing that it's coming, I still marvel at the illogical nature of that kind of statement, the completely unfounded but seemingly universal belief among nosy strangers trying to make conversation that boys as a gender are inherently and uniformly less complicated, more loving, better children than are girls. And I am never prepared for the fact that people feel compelled to tell me these things right in front of my daughter.

"Everyone's allowed to have meltdowns, girls *and* boys," I tell the nurse after a shocked pause, knowing my daughter is listening. It's weak, but in the moment I am unable to come up with anything better.

The nurse looks confused, and then it dawns on her: I just don't know yet. "Boys love their mothers differently than girls," she says as the elevator doors open. "You'll see!"

I wish her a good day and push the stroller into the waiting room of my OB's office, where my daughter immediately spies a jar of lollipops and forgets to be cranky.

Confession: I did not want to have a boy.

I am the oldest of three girls. When we were growing up, my parents often joked about how they really wanted boys and just kept trying until it was obvious it wasn't going to happen. My mother talked about how they had been so sure I was going to be a boy, they hadn't even considered a girl's name. She told me many times how, when I was first born, the doctors said, "It's a boy! No, wait, it's a girl! No, a boy! No, it's definitely a girl!" (the kind of story any girl definitely wants to hear again and again as she hits puberty). The name they ended up giving me is suspiciously masculine. After I left for college, my mother started taking in foreign exchange students—boys. The annual family holiday newsletter (written, of course, in rhyme) invariably included glowing paragraphs of updates on the wondrous accomplishments of "our sons."

All of this cumulatively sealed the deal for me: If I was going to have a baby, it would be a girl. I did not want to be the mother of a boy. I would want a girl and have a girl, and I would not tell her stories about how she looked just like the boy in her favorite movie, *The Black Stallion*, or that if she cut her hair really short, no one would be able to tell she wasn't a boy. My baby would be a girl, and I would be happy about that.

When I was pregnant with my daughter, I knew right from the beginning she was Emily, the girl I'd planned on having. It was no surprise to me when the ultrasound confirmed that belief. I'd had girl feelings, girl dreams, girl convictions from the start. Of course she was a girl: That was what I wanted.

When I discovered I was pregnant the second time around, I hoped for another girl. I had visions of having two daughters, of seeing that special sister bond recreated in the next generation of my family. But I wasn't as sure as I had been the first time. I had one baby dream early on in the pregnancy, and it was of giving birth to a boy. In the dream, he came out blond and big and more coordinated than a newborn really is; within minutes of giving birth, my room was populated with all the mothers I know in real life who have sons, all of them holding their boy babies and smirking at me because they knew I'd really wanted a girl. One of them asked me, "What's his name?" and I realized I didn't have a name for him. "Can you believe it?" the dream mothers said to one another. "She doesn't even have a name picked out!" I started to panic. Before I woke up, I looked at my nameless boy baby and thought, *At least he looks like* Emi. The dream logic was, evidently, that if he at least looked like his sister, it might make it easier to deal with the fact that he wasn't a girl himself.

Even after this dream, I stuck to my conviction that I was having another girl. I contemplated girl names. I painted the baby's room lavender. But inwardly I began to doubt my firm girl-only stance. The dream nagged at me. I didn't have the same fierce girl feelings I had had when I was pregnant with my daughter. I began to grudgingly acknowledge the possibility that this baby could be a boy.

At my nineteen-week ultrasound, the tech took her time, checking the kidneys, the heart, the legs, the head. She asked us if we wanted to know whether the baby was a girl or a boy, and I joked, "Yes, but only if it's a girl." She said she couldn't really get a great view, so she had the doctor come in and take a look.

"Well, look at that!" he said, right away. "Get a load of that scrotum!"

"What?" I choked back my surprise as I craned my neck trying to look at the grainy image on the screen. My husband gripped my hand tightly, warning me with his eyes that a freak-out would not be the most appropriate response.

"Yep, that's a penis! We're looking at a boy, here!" The doctor's smile turned to an expression of concern as he tilted his head over to look at me. "Mom? Are we okay with this?"

My husband squeezed my hand tighter and looked at the doctor. He said, through gritted teeth, "She's crying because she's so happy."

It took me a few weeks to wrap my brain around the idea that I was carrying a boy baby inside me, that in a few months he would come out into the world and I would be a mother of a son. I had to practice smiling as I said, "It's a boy," when people would ask me whether I was having a boy or a girl. I had to find a way to hide my unbidden tears of disappointment when strangers would begin the litany of how much more I would love my son, how much more devoted sons are than daughters.

"A boy! Now you've got a rich man's family!" more than one person told me.

"Now you can stop," said someone else. ("Stop what?" I asked, confused. "Stop having kids!" was the reply.)

"Boys are so much easier than girls! You'll just love having a boy!" said just about everyone.

But I wasn't sure.

What if I loved him less? I worried. But then I realized that my real fear was that—just like all the strangers seemed to imply, just like my parents' unrealized wish for a son had seemed to imply—I might love him more:

I might love him more deeply, more intensely, more wholeheartedly than I loved my daughter, and I'd leave her behind—loved, like I feared I was, a little less, simply because she is a girl.

I remember being about eight or nine when someone, for the hundredth time, asked me and my sisters what we wanted to be when we grew up. We looked at each other, not really knowing what to say, since we knew that fanciful answers would get us teased and serious answers would be greeted with skepticism. Finally, I said, "Just a mom, I guess." My sisters agreed. I remember the look on my mom's face, a mix of surprise and disappointment, and how she took a beat before she said, brightly, "That's right, I always told my girls they could be anything they wanted to be, even mommies," and moved us on to another topic.

I could tell she was surprised that we didn't ask for more, even disappointed that at such an early age, we saw right through her: She might have been a teacher, a small-town theater actress, an indefatigable supporter of and chauffeur for all our extracurricular activities, but despite all that, she was still just a mom.

Perhaps that's one reason our relationships with our daughters are more complicated than our relationships with our sons: We are conflicted. We want our daughters to do everything our sons do, yet as mothers ourselves, we know the difficulties and the hard choices they will have to make when they grow up and choose to mother—the career options that dwindle; the daily balancing act that exhausts; the kind of things our sons will never face, even as they become parents themselves. Perhaps it's easier to love our sons because there is no big secret, no truth we're withholding about the divided life of women. Perhaps we feel less conflicted about boys—love them more, believe they love us differently than our daughters do—because they will have such unconflicted, uncomplicated autonomy as men.

But whenever someone insists to me that girls are more "complicated" than boys, I can't help but wonder whether or not that insistence of complication in fact creates a complicated relationship. "Complicated" seems to be a code word for "harder to love." And yet what love is always easy, and who can say which kind means more?

"It's a love affair," a mother of a son tells me, gesturing to the boy baby babbling on her lap, leaning into her shoulder, indeed, like a lover. But it feels wrong to me, this boy love. It feels as though I am being told to love a boy because he is my link to power, to empowerment, to unencumbered motion through the world. It feels as though I am being told that girls remind us how we are constricted by our gender; that boys set us free.

These are the questions I have, the things I wonder about after I have these boy versus girl conversations with strangers. Do we force this dichotomy, thinking of boys as "easy" and girls as "hard," romanticizing our sons and seeing our daughters as rivals? Or are boys really easier, is it pure biochemistry? Are boys simply engineered from a more manageable hormone than estrogen?

"Boys love their mothers differently," the nurse assured me that day as she watched me wrestle with my complicated daughter. But I think she had it wrong: Maybe mothers love their boys differently, not the other way around.

A few weeks after having my gender-predicting dream confirmed by the ultrasound, I lay in bed one night, on my left side like a good pregnant woman, and thought about the baby inside me, whom I could already feel as a hard knot pushing this way and that in my rounded belly. I tried to relax my mind and, as my yoga instructor might say, just be there, feeling the baby move, thinking about him as a boy. *Who will he look like?* I wondered. *What kind of temperament will he have? What kind of person will he be?*

In the dark there, I felt a rush of emotion followed by a feeling of complete stillness, and then, suddenly, the sense that everything was going to be okay. I imagined that, just for a moment, I had been able to sense the essence of the little being inside me. For that fleeting minute, I knew more than his sex: I felt as though I knew who he was. I knew he would be curious, I knew he would be funny, I knew he would be mellow, I knew he would be loving; I knew he would love me the way all babies, boys or girls, love their mothers. And I knew that I would be able to love him fully right back.

He is here, now, two years old. I have my "rich man's family," as advertised. And I'm finding that I do love my son differently than I loved my daughter—some days, even more easily, as I can't deny that his particular temperament (something not tied to gender, I believe) sure does make him easy to love. But I do not love him differently because he is a boy. I love him differently because I am different this time. With this second child, I am more sure of myself. I am less tentative, more expansive. I am more ready to surrender to motherhood, more willing to embrace this time in my life and the work I must do in it. And maybe that's what makes the kind of love I have for my son different from the hesitant, fearful, intense love I had for my daughter: Not his boyness, but the fact that I've had practice. Not his boyness, but my readiness now to give myself over to difficult, messy, complicated, heartbreaking, heart-bursting love for both of my children, girl and boy alike.

You've Got Male!

JODY
MACE

When I was pregnant with my second child, I bought two matching colorful sundresses for my children to wear the next summer. One in a size 4, for my daughter, who would be three when she became a big sister, and one in a size 9 months for the baby. I had the picture all planned out mentally: Kyla would patiently hold her little sister's hand, as the spirited toddler tried to walk off. They'd be wearing white hats. No, straw hats. Maybe they'd be barefoot. I love barefoot children. The baby was called "Caroline."

I didn't seriously entertain the possibility that the new baby could be a boy.

Soon after, I had an ultrasound, and, predictably, it featured a penis. I tried to explain it away. "Maybe her hand is down there and that's a finger."

The ultrasound technician didn't have to take a second glance at the picture. "That's no finger."

I had never pictured myself as the mother of boys. It sounds terrible, I know, to be disappointed about the gender of your unborn child, and "disappointed" probably isn't the right word. You're disappointed when you're getting something that you're familiar with and you don't want it. That wasn't the case. I was getting something unknown. It was as if the ultrasound technician had said, "Congratulations, Mrs. Mace, you're having a space alien."

I thought that I had a handle on little girls. At Kyla's preschool, I watched the little girls play. They drew charming pictures of awkwardly grinning families that dwarfed houses and trees. On the playground, they made elaborate feasts out of rocks and twigs to share with their friends, or they could be found playing Follow the Leader in a line. There seemed to be a purpose to their play that I could understand.

I did a writing project with the kids, in which they dictated stories for me to write down and then illustrated them.

This was a typical story from a girl:

"The little star was high up in the sky. At dark the little star was happy and he made friends. Then they played. The little star was having fun. They played tag. The little star had lots of friends. Then all of his friends and the little star went to school. They ate marshmallows."

Whereas the boys' stories generally were like this one:

"The monster tore down their house. And then tore down their head. And then the monster was sleeping in the bed. And then he broke the fountain. And then he cut off their legs. And then the monster bumped into a skeleton and he threw the skeleton out the door. And then he cut off their eyes. And the skeleton punched off their heads. They punched their arms off and bited their arms off. And then somebody else moved in. And then the skeleton tore down the other house. And then bited off their ears. Then they punched their mouth off. Then they punched their neck off. Then the monster stepped on the guy and shmushed him. And then a strong wrestler came. And then he threw the monster out the door and he went outside and he shmushed him and punched his head. The End."

It was all blood and guts, monsters, death, and destruction. And they were four! I didn't know how to react to such aggressive images in their writing and artwork. The strangest thing to me was that their parents were uniformly delighted with their young sons' creations. I didn't get it.

A big thing for the girls was playing house. It wasn't always pretty, but at least I could understand what they were doing.

GIRL 1: I'm the mommy. I'll give you a blanket and tuck you into bed.

GIRL 2: I am not going to be the baby again. [crosses arms]

GIRL 1: Then I'm not inviting you to my birthday party!

It wasn't that I liked this sort of verbal power play, but I did understand it. Because of this, I was able to talk to Kyla about it, and try to teach her to be kinder with her friends. While the girls were testing the social waters and uninviting friends to their parties, the boys were running around, hollering about Power Rangers, and sliding in the dirt. There was nothing charming or comprehensible to me about the way they played. I didn't even know what a Power Ranger was, but I was fairly certain I didn't want one at my birthday party.

I was relieved to find that a baby is a baby. Other than treating his penis as a loaded weapon during diaper changes, I didn't have to do anything different than I had done with Kyla. During that "babies are babies" time, I started to believe that the Power Ranger boys' wild behavior was due to poor parenting. I was gentle with Charlie. When he clawed my face, I took his hand and guided it in tender strokes on my cheek. "Gentle hands, gentle hands."

Soon he mimicked me and stroked my face gently.

When he was angry, I empathized with his feelings and gave him words to use. He was one sweet toddler. I also decided that I wasn't going to force him to fit into gender roles. When he put on a blue tutu and joined his sister in an impromptu and clumsy ballet in the living room, I applauded enthusiastically. In addition to the trucks that he adored, he had dolls that he nurtured. He lifted his shirt to feed them, and he was heart-broken when he learned from his informative older sister that he would never be able to breastfeed.

"Then what are these for?" he demanded, pulling on his nipples.

"Decoration?" I suggested.

He looked down at them critically. "So they won't grow into breastiss?"

"No, sweetheart, but boys have nice parts too."

When he discovered those nice parts, he started to figure out that being a boy had its advantages. I was fascinated and shocked at the same time by his "penis experiments," as he called them. I never dreamed that a foreskin could be stretched to such outrageous lengths. Of course I told him that future experiments should be carried out in private, but I couldn't help secretly being a bit won over by his enthusiasm for his nice boy parts.

Before having a son, when I heard of boys' fascinations with their gen-itals, it always seemed crude. But now with my own son, it was innocent and endearing. I got a kick out of his sense of discovery. Why shouldn't he be a bit obsessed by such an unlikely and wondrous thing on his body?

For the first time, though, I had a sense of otherness about my son. He was always a child whom I understood. I understood his moods. I got why he cried when the chocolate pudding ran out. I could anticipate what he would say. His facial expressions were a breeze to read. When he was frustrated, it was never a mystery to me why. We had a deep connec-tion to each other. But all of a sudden, there was this thing that he was experiencing that I had never experienced. I didn't know what it felt like to be a boy. The surprising thing was how his otherness, his boyness, was irresistible to me.

Anatomy was just the tip of the iceberg. Sometimes his solutions to problems, even at age four, were just so male. One day he was building block towers and they kept falling down. I helped him a couple of times but was tired of it. So I told him, "You're a highly capable person. You'll figure it out," and I left the room. When I came back in, he had rebuilt the tower and secured the blocks together with duct tape. Apparently the "duct tape" part of the Y chromosome kicks in early.

And Charlie became scarily similar to the Power Ranger boys from Kyla's preschool. No, he didn't know about the Power Rangers (no violent TV for my Charlie!), but no matter. He played in exactly the same way. Most of his games involved chasing or being chased, wrestling, and hollering. Spinning around until he had to stagger around dizzily also figured prominently in his play, as did putting things like trash cans on his head and walking into walls. Several times he inexplicably got his head stuck in the banister. I've never known a girl to do that. As he developed verbally, he became fond of potty humor and knock-knock jokes without sensible punch lines. In short, he did every unfathomable thing that I had ever distastefully noticed little boys doing. Strangely, however, when he did those things I found them cute.

His energy was appealing to me. It was as if there was a force of nature pulsating inside of him, and his body wasn't big enough or coordinated enough to control it yet. While Kyla skipped and leapt and landed like a cat, Charlie lumbered and hurtled, and tripped over himself like a puppy that hadn't yet grown into its feet.

And yet that tenderness that I had tried so hard to nurture was still there, and maybe that was the most irresistible thing of all. He'd run across the room, hunched over a dump truck, making *vroom!* noises, so fast and recklessly that he'd fall headfirst over the truck. And in the next moment, he'd kiss me on the cheek and look meaningfully into my eyes. And then he'd go careening off again. It was that juxtaposition of tough and tender, of rough and gentle, that was so moving to me.

I think a lot about the man that Charlie will become. It's strange to imagine that in just a few years, he will tower over me. I can't seem to get used to the fact that one day I'll be the mother to a man, and that somewhere within that man will be the wild little boy who barreled through the house with a dump truck, and the tender boy who pretended to nurse his dolls. Maybe that's part of the appeal of being the mother of a boy: the chance to plant something gentle in his soul, to give the future a small gift—a man who can be as loving as he is strong.

Exile in Boyville

MARRIT
INGMAN

Everything changed on my son's second Christmas.

Where once there had been unisex onesies and bibs gaily painted with smiling fruit, there were plaid golfer's pants and a three-piece suit with a coordinating bow tie. Where once there had been fuzzy stuffed giraffes and cloth books, there were Bob the Builder talking machines and a toy Dodge Viper the size of a shoe box. It screamed out the sounds of burning rubber and an Yngwie Malmsteen cock-rock guitar riff. And there was a Little People playset, a tableau of demolition with a wrecking ball and blocks.

Even without the batteries, Baldo preferred his machines to the toys I liked: the *djembe* made from a vinegar jug, the shoe-box guitar, the alphabet blocks. He screamed to hold our electric leaf blower. A passing glance at a neighbor's lawnmower would send him into car seat paroxysms. His bedtime stories were all set in the hardware department at Sears.

"Why don't Nee-Nee Robot and Dee-Dee Robot go to the library?" I'd implore.

"Go Sears! Go Sears! Get nails!" he'd insist.

"All right," I sighed, and once more Baldo's imaginary robot friends hung sheetrock in their bathroom.

It was true what the obstetrician had said. It was a boy.

More to the point, my son seemed to be a guy. I knew little boys who liked to play with feather dusters and watch synchronized swimming. I knew little boys who loved to play dress-up in heels and nail polish, who caused their conservative parents grief. Wouldn't I—an open-minded feminist mother with relaxed ideas about gender—be better able to nurture such a free-spirited little soul?

Yet as it turned out, I wasn't as open-minded as I thought I was. And I wasn't as relaxed about gender as I thought I was. Because when my son showed signs of guyness, it drove me up the wall.

We spoke not the word "football," but he learned it just the same. Another mom showed up for a playdate with a pigskin in her hand. My son seized it promptly, and despite my vigilance, the football was left behind in our yard. It became an object of mystery, this "Brad ball." Baldo threw lima beans across the length of our kitchen in a nice, tight spiral. "Brad ball!" he'd yell.

I could only sigh. I envisioned myself years from now in a booster club t-shirt with a folding padded stadium chair, cheering not for the woodwind section but for a grizzled gridiron hero who toilet-papered cheerleaders' houses and hazed the junior varsity.

I grew up in a house of women; it was like a Fellini film. A sister, a mother, a grandmother next door, a female dog and cats. My best friends were three sisters at the end of the block. We listened to ABBA and Olivia

Newton-John on the radio. The ladies from the garden club and PTA met at our house, smoking Eve menthols around the kitchen table, and my mom led a Girl Scout troop. We were femmes. The sole butch presence was my father: prone to napping; emotionally detached; Jeep driving; obsessed with *Wide World of Sports*, which he watched while seemingly asleep in the leather chair that was *his*. A soap-on-a-rope kind of guy—grew up playing baseball, likes *Equipment Trader* and farm auctions. I don't live in his world, and it frightens me sometimes. I love the man, but he drives a dually truck with a bumper sticker that reads, BEEF. IT'S WHAT'S FOR DINNER.

Some people don't have this problem. "I dug all that boy stuff," said my friend Robin, a mother of one boy. "I guess I embraced all the things that I didn't get to do or play with growing up a girl—Matchbox cars, playing fireman, shoot 'em up games."

I consulted *Kick Me: Adventures in Adolescence*, a lively memoir by Paul Feig, to learn more about the world of boys. Feig is the creator of the short-lived cult TV show *Freaks and Geeks* and the star of young adult films such as *Heavyweights*, the story of a fat camp. Feig's book is like a Disneyland jungle cruise through junior high boyhood: a dog pile in the locker room here, masturbatory sensations while climbing a rope there. Feig seems to have been one of those sensitive boy souls, the one picked last for team sports, the one who liked to wear slacks to school instead of jeans and dress up in his mother's go-go boots. Of course he got his ass kicked. Perhaps he wasn't the best guide to mysterious Boy World, but his stories are terrifyingly candid. Perhaps my son would instead grow up to be like Karl Scott, the twelve-year-old bully who pelted Feig with dodge balls in gym class.

When I talked to Paul Feig by phone, he told me, "There are other things that aren't in the book. I took ballet for a long time when I was a kid, tap dancing when I was in junior high. It leaked out somehow that I was in ballet. Talk about not being 'in.'"

"What happened?" I asked.

"What do you think?" he rejoined. "It's always the guys you don't want to have know about that who find out. In one way I was immune to it because it happened so much, but in another way it always crushed me. It's such a debilitating blow when people make fun of you."

I nodded. Since the stick turned pink, I'd been preparing myself for the day when a son of mine came home from school in tears or got socked in the eye at the playground, called "pussy" or "fag." I'd been girding myself to defend Baldo's choice of a purple sweater or a fairy-princess Halloween costume. "My son is an individual!" the imaginary maternal Me proclaimed. (She's so feisty.) While the rest of the parents in my suburban neighborhood celebrated team sports and NASCAR, I'd root for the Drama Club or Mu Alpha Theta. I'd foster his interest in synthesizer programming or pointillism. I'd show him how to spike his hair, use lip liner, and deconstruct his t-shirts. We would stand arm in arm against the forces of conformity and essentialism. We'd watch *Hedwig* together.

There was one small problem. I'd made all these decisions about who my son was going to be without consulting him.

I watched him stack three blocks on his Little People demolition set, aligning the corners just *so*. Then he deployed the pretend plunger, toppling the tower. "This is my *boomstick!*" he cried. His father had introduced him to *Army of Darkness*, and the boy took to it like a duck to water.

"I expected to have a kid who wanted to play dress-up and who was sensitive and who was subcultural or whatever," I told Feig. "But he likes football. He likes Black Sabbath. And he's only two."

"Oh my God!" he blurted.

"I don't know how to handle his masculine aptitude," I confessed.

"I always feel weird saying this because I don't have kids," he said, "but I think it's all about just letting kids see what everybody else is going through. Just put yourself in another person's head. It's really just about exposing him to as much stuff as you can. That said, you may be stuck with a big guy. Especially when you're a kid you naturally go toward what your parents hate."

This seemed reasonable.

Katherine Gould, a mother of two girls from Los Angeles and author of *A Tiger in the Bedroom: Lessons from Mother Nature's Sex Shop*, told me, "I was always a trucks and mud kind of girl, and I figured I could steer my daughters toward trucks and trains to make sure they had a balance of play choices." She added, "They want to dress up as princesses, have tea parties, and set up elaborate games with their dolls."

Or maybe it's just the luck of the draw. Bee Lavender, mother of two from Seattle and publisher of *Hip Mama*, says, "My son wears suits and ties, plays chess, and prefers to listen to books on tape instead of going outside. He is a studious and serious small gentleman. This has been surprising and interesting, and I don't take any credit for his choices."

As I listened to these other people, it finally started to become clear: Like so many parents, I'd been investing too much of my own identity in my developing child, thinking of him as a mirror whose only job was to reflect my values. I needed to learn to accept him unconditionally, to delight in his discoveries because they pleased him—not me.

This didn't mean I'd have to jettison my own personality: I'd still have a thing or two to say about toy crossbows, talk radio punditry, and Donald Rumsfeld. I could deconstruct my own t-shirts. For neither was I a mirror to my son, an adoring visage who smiled at his every word.

Even though he is barely two years old, we have already begun the dance of separation, the give-and-take of two loving people struggling to stand beside one another come what may. I danced this way before, with my own parents, when I grew up to be a lit major; when instead of a rugged West Texas cowboy, I fell in love with a Californian with hay fever and lactose intolerance.

I call upon this history now as I await my son's second birthday, the day after tomorrow. One box, from his grandparents, contains a train set. Another gift, from his father, is an assortment of miniature cars, including a Hummer. My present is a stacking toy with wooden pieces that fit together to make the head and body of a clown. I chose something whimsical yet kinesthetic, something appealing but essentially genderless. Aren't clowns essentially people in drag? People in masks? People who are comfortable wearing lipstick and wigs, driving miniature cars, and being wacky? My stacking clown is a gift, I hope, for both of us: a puzzle to conquer for him, and a reminder to me of the possibilities—even if I am, at heart, a coulrophobe.

Son of a Guy

ONA
GRITZ

Six weeks after I separated from my husband, I went to Washington, D.C., to join the Million Mom March in support of sensible gun laws. There, at the National Mall, as I stood in the crowd listening to speeches, I was distracted by a three-year-old boy (okay, my three-year-old boy) who had picked up a stick and was pretending to shoot us all with it.

Though I took the stick away quickly and did my best to redirect my son, I was convinced that everyone around us—all those wonderful, politically active, pacifist moms—was staring at us and forming opinions on the kind of mother I was. Clearly, they believed I raised my child on action adventure movies, combat video games, and violent toys. But, honestly, this couldn't be further from the truth.

At the time, Ethan owned books, toy trains and cars, stuffed animals, and even a couple of baby dolls. He had never seen a violent video game, and his word for television was not "TV" but "PBS."

So where, then, did this attraction to violent play come from? Years ago I decided that gender differences were foisted upon us by a limiting culture. When I had my son, I still held those beliefs, but before long I realized that male aggressiveness was simply part of who he was. It was in him. And my only explanation for how it got there was that his father was a guy.

I don't mean it's because his father was male. Obviously all fathers are male, and many of them have gentle, docile children of both genders. Ethan's father, my ex, was a guy guy.

It was, in part, Matt's guy qualities that first drew me to him. He was strong, good looking, and athletic. Just the type of guy who would have looked right through me in high school. I found his interest in me flattering. And at twenty-one, he was really openhearted. Though his outward persona was of a wild boy and a jock, when we were alone he liked to sweet-talk and cuddle, a side he never let any of his friends see.

In fact, Matt believed a guy couldn't become really good friends with another guy unless they'd had a physical fight first. His own best friend from college had challenged him to a wrestling match the day they met. Matt broke Chris's collarbone, and they have been close ever since.

All of Matt's friends were devoted to each other, but in the twelve years I lived with Matt, I never heard them have anything I recognized as a conversation. They spoke to each other in a code that, from the outside, sounded like insults.

"Hey, asshole," Matt could often be heard saying into the phone. To which I assume the person on the other end responded in kind.

"You should have seen him as a kid," his family was fond of telling me. It seems every boy on his block was, at one time or another, not allowed to play with him. He was known for getting into fights and for inventing games—such as blindfolded bike riding—that often resulted in broken bones.

Property wasn't safe either. His aunt's favorite anecdote involved coming over to the house and finding him breaking up the front steps with a hammer.

Despite all this, when I imagined the kind of child we would one day have, I pictured a girl much like myself. I had been a quiet, agreeable, soft-spoken child. According to both my parents, I had been easy.

When the technician at my ultrasound told me I was having a boy, I knew I was in trouble. At first I didn't believe her.

"Are you sure?" I asked. After all, I had heard stories in which the umbilical chord was mistaken for a penis.

But her response was, "I'd bet my house on it."

This stunned me. I was supposed to have a girl. A little me. Even Matt seemed surprised.

"Oh, boy," he sighed. "Batten down the hatches."

And when we told Matt's family, they responded with a jostling "Payback time!"

Sure, payback for him. But what did I ever do?

Still, part of me was happy with the news. This person wasn't even born yet, and he had already busted my preconceptions about him. I felt proud of him for that. And as it turned out, Ethan was a beautiful, affectionate baby. In his first year, I didn't worry about any of this. I didn't really have time. He was so affectionate that he wanted to be held constantly, and only I was allowed to do the holding.

I was a nervous new mother, careful to handle him gently. But Ethan soon let me know that he himself had a rougher hand. He flung toys, slapped the floor when he crawled, and thought it hysterically funny to bump his head into things. On the padded floor of our Mommy & Me movement class, his favorite game was to sneak up behind me and yank me by the collar so that I tumbled onto my back. He would then pounce on my chest. I didn't mind that. In the earlier years of my marriage, I used to play wrestle with his dad, too. Plus Ethan's guy proclivities weren't constant. He also loved to cuddle and be read to and nurture "Baby Ethan," his look-alike doll.

Then came the infamous twos.

There's always one kid in every playgroup who will throw a toy car at an unsuspecting child's head. Or on the playground, see a girl carefully doing a balance beam walk along a ledge and shove her. That's my boy! I had to constantly rein in his aggressiveness. It baffled me. I couldn't relate to it at all.

I was really struggling, and at this point, my marriage was struggling too. Before Ethan was born, I was pretty comfortable with the fact that Matt and I had separate interests and social circles. I'd always been independent, so I didn't think of Matt as neglectful if he chose to go mountain biking rather than spend the weekend with me. I was just as happy to be with my women friends.

But now that we were parents together, I wanted more of a partner. He still went mountain biking on the weekends, while I stayed home to take care of Ethan. Now I did see this as his being neglectful of me and, even worse, our son. It really struck me hard when he went away for a ten-day bike tour and Ethan didn't ask for him once.

"You're just like the father in 'Cat's in the Cradle,'" I told him.

"You're using song lyrics against me?" Matt yelled. "You know what your problem is? You think with your emotions." I knew from previous fights that he saw this as an inexplicable female trait. "Women really are from another planet!" he shouted. I had to agree. He and I, at least, spoke different languages and experienced the world in opposing ways.

The argument continued until Matt finally got so frustrated he punched a hole in our living room door. Our fights didn't always escalate to the point where he hit something, but it happened often enough. I knew he would never hurt me or Ethan, but it was still a form of violence, and it scared me.

The next day I took Ethan to the library, where he threw a book at the librarian during story hour. That old question, "What did I ever do?" rang in my head, this time followed by an answer: I married the wrong guy.

So while I was extricating myself from this man I knew I could no longer live with, I had to reconcile the fact that one of the main qualities of his that made that true—his volatile nature—was also very much a part of the one person in the world I couldn't live without: my son.

It surprised me to discover how little I missed Matt once we separated. Like Ethan, I was used to not having him around. I felt free, and my days seemed charged with possibility. Even better was the fact that after the divorce, Matt became a much more attentive father. He lived close by and committed himself to staying involved in Ethan's life. Of course, that meant he stayed in my life, too. Though I was coming to realize that even if he hadn't, he would be there in the aggressive, short-tempered male I still lived with.

"I'll be paying for my bad taste in men for the rest of my life," I complained to a friend while Ethan led a wild rumpus worthy of Maurice Sendak's Max in synagogue one Saturday. We both burst out laughing, and the irreverence of making the remark out loud felt cathartic to me. But then I did what I had to do.

I marched up to Ethan and led him to a bench.

"Let's slow our breathing," I said, having discovered that this calms him.

We counted and breathed, and then he rested his head on my shoulder.

I thought about how I used to believe Matt's tender side would win out eventually. And when that didn't happen, I still thought that I could change him. I now knew how naive that had been. But in my relationship with Ethan, I was in charge and I could make changes. In fact, it was my job to do so.

I tend to believe that people come into your life for a reason. To me, Ethan is here in part to teach me what I wasn't able to learn as Matt's wife: to set boundaries. The largeness of Matt's nature overwhelmed me. That same largeness exists in Ethan, but in a much more manageable package. Throughout his preschool years, he gave me countless opportunities to learn how to curtail his spill of energy and aggressiveness.

At some point it clicked. He's eight now, a strong boy who is a leader in his classroom. He still has boundless energy, but he really has to be provoked for that energy to turn aggressive. His humor can include violence in a way that's unsettling to me, but I find he shares that with many of the boys in his class. Also, it's counterbalanced by a remarkably gentle side. He's sweet and affectionate with babies and toddlers in a way I never could have foreseen when he was a rambunctious toddler himself. And he has yet to outgrow being outwardly loving toward me: As concerned as he is about acting cool among his friends, he'll still call out, "I love you!" before I leave him at school and kiss my hand while we're walking down the street.

I used to worry that I was the wrong person to adequately meet the needs of a high-energy boy. Little old bookish me with no comprehension of Yu-Gi-Oh cards or Game Boy or many of his latest passions. But there are lots of activities we do share. And of course the one thing I did learn by being Matt's wife is to never set aside my own separate interests. This saved my sanity and helped our marriage survive long enough to result in our little boy. Now our co-parenting arrangement has allowed me to return to the pursuits that fuel me. As a result, I find I'm able to be more present during the time I am with Ethan.

It has also allowed me the time to nurture a new relationship. Ethan and I now live with an artist named Ed, who is not a guy guy. He's soft-spoken and enjoys meaningful conversation. However, he and Ethan do have something in common (which supports my belief that men really are by nature different creatures than women): They both find fart jokes really funny.

Though Matt and I never became friendly enough after our separation to share other parts of our lives, we are good at co-parenting. Once in a while, we even seek each other out to commiserate about our boy.

"I don't see myself in Ethan much at all," he told me recently.

"Come on," I responded. But then I thought about it. Unlike his father, Ethan has no interest in sports. Matt argues that Ethan needs sports as an outlet for his aggressive energy, but Ethan has found other outlets that work for him. Drawing calms him the most.

And there's something else. Ethan is surprisingly articulate about his feelings. I believe this helps prevent him from getting overtaken by them. He's very sensitive. In fact, it could even be said that he "thinks with his emotions."

It makes me wonder. I know Matt loves Ethan as much as I do, and for that I'm grateful. But maybe he also looks at our son at times and thinks, *I'll be paying for my bad taste in women for the rest of my life.*

A Son's Love

CAROLINE
LEAVITT

When I got pregnant in my forties, I was so ecstatic, so thrilled that I was able to be pregnant at my age, that I honestly didn't care what the sex of my child was.

That is, not until they told me.

"You're carrying a girl," my friends assured me, patting my round belly. "Boys are carried lower and you gain around the hips."

"Girl," assured my mother. "It runs in our family."

I started to get excited, to rattle off names I loved: Chloe and Ruby and Lily Rose. I began to imagine a daughter I'd shield from all the things that had bothered me. I'd teach her to value herself over magazine images. I'd encourage her to be independent, to know she could be anything she wanted. And I'd instruct her that when she was ready to fall in love, she should fall in love with funny rather than handsome, with kind rather than life of the party. In short, I'd teach her all the things I wished someone had taught me.

The day of my amniocentesis, my husband and I held hands. "Ah, clear as champagne," said the doctor as he drew the fluid up the needle. Then they did an ultrasound. We stared at the monitor. A blurry image, a starfish in deep, murky waters, floated by. I couldn't see a thing. "What is it?" I asked, but what I really meant was, *Show me my girl.* The doctor grinned. "Penis!" he cried, and pointed it out, a small angular bulb swimming on the screen, and suddenly, to my horror, my eyes filled with disappointed tears.

A boy? My Ruby/Chloe/Lily was a boy?

Everything began to suddenly change. My "Girls are great" friends started to be replaced by mothers with boys. "Boys grow up and buy their mothers houses," one friend assured me.

"You don't see people fighting for the honor of their fathers, do you?" another said. "But say 'Your mama' and all hell breaks loose."

I nodded, trying to take comfort. But my mind was suddenly a neighborhood where I didn't know the people or the customs, and I wasn't quite sure I knew how to live in it. All my shopping scenarios, my little frilly dresses, my mother-daughter heart-to-heart talks were replaced by visions of baseball and roughhousing.

And then, my son Max Henry Leavitt Tamarkin was born and I fell in love, head over heels.

No, he wasn't the little girl of my dreams, but he wasn't the little boy of those pregnancy-time dreams either. My friend Linda, who had a boy, handed down all the items she was sure he was hard-wired for: Tonka trucks and water pistols. My friend Elinor told me, sighing, "Boys don't communicate the way girls do, but if you trap them in a car ride, you can get stuff out of them."

"Boys are different, there's nothing you can do about it," said my friend Janet flatly.

Janet was right. But not in the way she thought. Max ignored the trucks and kicked the pistols under the bed. He snuggled in our laps and talked about everything, his voice rising and falling like music. Yes, he loves sports, but he also cries when he sees a teammate hurt. He won't sit still like the quieter girls in his class do, but he can read for hours, insisting on bringing his book to the table. And as he grows, as I watch him, the scenario of having a girl to whom I could give all the things I had missed changes, and I begin to see a boy who's giving me things I never realized were possible. A boy who's changing my feelings about what a boy is, and what it means to raise one. I am loving him differently than I would my imagined daughter, differently than I had imagined I would love a son.

Guiltily, I approach my friends. I adore my husband, but this feeling, this falling in love with my son this way, is something I never expected. Am I one of those horrible Jewish mothers so in love with their sons they smother them? Am I going to hate his girl- (or boy-) friends because I want to be first in his heart? I tell my friends, "Whoever he falls in love with is going to thank me." It's strange, this feeling, as if I'm a mad scientist creating the perfect man. A dash of sensitivity, a soupçon of good humor, dollops and dollops of affection. And sometimes it makes me sad, because sooner than later, another woman, or man, will be the apple of my son's eye. Another person will share his secrets and hold his hand. I try to think of something imperfect about him, and all I can think of is he doesn't brush his teeth long enough.

"Are you in love with your son?" I shyly ask my friend Rochelle, who laughs and says, "Of course, I am."

"Are you in love with your boy?" I ask Jane, who nods. "Absolutely," she says. What is it, this bond between mother and son?

"You can't know that it would have been different with a girl. And you can't know if it would have been different with a different boy than our Max," my husband tells me.

And he's right. Because it's this boy, this son, that I am so enraptured by. This boy who makes me willing to turn myself inside out for him, and makes me repeat, "I'm so lucky, I'm so lucky," like a mantra. It's not that his love is different because he's a boy. Or that mine is different because I'm his mother loving him. It's that he is who he is. Nothing like anyone I ever expected. A revelation. Just like my love for him.

My Three Sons

JENNIFER
MARGULIS

As the youngest of four children and the only girl, I longed for an older sister. My brothers from my mother's first marriage were ten and eight years older than I. They were sullen teenagers who grew pot in the attic closet, set bomb scares at high school, and sneaked girls up the back stairs into their rooms. They taught me how to blow bubbles in their bongs and let my youngest brother Zach and me jump frantically on their unmade beds while they blasted Alice Cooper's "School's Out" at earsplitting volume. I grew up in a house of three boys, one man, and a mother—a microbiologist—who spent all of her time in a man's world.

When I got pregnant, I knew from the day of conception that I was having a girl. My husband and I were so excited that we chattered to the baby, played Bach concertos with headphones on my belly before its ears were even formed, sang it French lullabies with what we thought were clever English translations, and made plans for it over my burgeoning belly. We read our lists of boys' and girls' names to it and tried to decide by the number of kicks which ones the baby preferred.

James would pretend the baby talked to him. One day he cupped his hand over his ear on my belly.

"Really?" he said.

"What?"

"It's a secret," James answered. "But now I know if we're having a boy or a girl."

"Tell me!" I cried. James knew I was sure it was a girl.

"I can't," he told me. "I promised the baby I wouldn't tell. Besides, you're the one who didn't want to find out in the first place." So we made a compromise—he wrote down what the baby had told him on a piece of paper, which he hid in a sealed envelope.

"Dear Chickpea," I wrote that night in the journal we had started for the baby. "You're already keeping secrets from Mommy."

In the first seconds after the baby was born, I looked into its tiny face and realized it *was* a boy. The baby's ears stuck out at right angles like my husband's, and its calm, inquisitive eyes looked exactly like his. For a second I felt a stab of disappointment. Then, sobbing with relief at having survived a grueling twenty-two-hour labor, I rearranged my feelings and adjusted to having become the mother of a son. It was then that I looked fully at my baby's tiny naked body and saw the irrefutable evidence that she was a girl. I felt disappointed again—but only for a moment. I realized I had the daughter I had always wanted.

Months later I found the sealed envelope. On the slip of paper inside, in his spidery almost illegible hand, James had written Boy.

The hot July day in Atlanta that my son—who turned out to be my daughter—was born was the day I became a mother. But that pregnancy was not my first.

At the beginning of the school year, a month after I turned twenty-one, I was seized by nausea during dance class. We were doing outdoor improvisation, leaping over boulders and twirling across the college lawns. I made gagging motions, clenching my stomach, pretending to put a finger down my throat. My dance partner, who was supposed to mirror my movements, looked at me like I was crazy.

It took me two weeks to figure out that I needed a pregnancy test.

"Congratulations. It's positive," a nurse from the clinic told me when I answered the phone on a Friday afternoon. I sobbed so hard I dropped the receiver. I wanted to have children more than anything else in my life, but my boyfriend and I were having a hard time in a long-distance relationship that was fraught with tension. Max was dividing his time between a difficult job teaching Spanish to inner-city kids in New York and taking care of his father, who was dying of lung cancer, in New Jersey. I was in California studying for a master's in comparative literature. Instead of being open and supportive with each other, we were jealous and secretive. Our relationship, even long distance, was choking me. More than that, I desperately did not want to repeat my mother's mistakes. She married at nineteen and had my oldest brother when she was twenty-one. The day before her wedding, she recorded a tape of all the reasons her fiancé wasn't right for her, and all the reasons she shouldn't marry him. I wanted my children to have a caring and attentive father, but, like my mother and her first husband, Max and I were so mired in competitiveness and defensiveness that I knew we could never parent together effectively.

I called my mother to tell her I was pregnant and that I was going to have an abortion. She was sorry that I was in tears, but she couldn't understand why I was so upset. "Oh Jenny," she said, her voice betraying a hint of exasperation. "It's like cutting your fingernails." That weekend

I hid, sick with shame and nausea, under the covers on my futon on the cold floor in the ragtag apartment my brother Zach and I shared. I spoke to no one but my brother all weekend, screaming and sobbing at him until he promised me he would not tell anyone, not even his girlfriend, that I was pregnant.

Since my menstrual cycles were so irregular and I wasn't sure when the fetus had been conceived, a few days later I had a sonogram.

"You don't have to look at the screen," said the overweight, short-haired physician's assistant who scheduled it. My aunt, my father's sister, lived in Berkeley and accompanied me to the appointment. I remember she nodded her head knowingly. But I had no idea what a sonogram was, what the screen was for, what I didn't have to look at. So I looked. What I saw was the outline of a baby, not the clump of unformed cells that I expected.

"We have two kinds of medication we can give you." My doctor had curly blond hair and a kind face. She was diminutive, almost childlike in stature, but as she prepped me for the abortion, she spoke in a clinical way that bespoke competence. "One is like strong aspirin; it will take most of the pain away. The other doesn't lessen the pain so much as it makes you forget it afterward."

"No!" I could hear myself shouting, though I hadn't meant to. "Don't give me that. I don't want anything that will make me forget."

My feet were buckled into stirrups, my legs bent, my vulva and anus completely exposed to the doctor and the nurse, whose probes and machines made unsettling sucking and whirring noises. I turned my face away and squeezed my aunt's hand.

"Everything's fine, everything's great. We're almost done here," the doctor's voice was soothing. "Try to relax." A minute later I felt cold creeping into my body, numbing my face and stiffening my limbs.

"Dr. Spawner," the nurse cried suddenly, nudging the doctor to look at the heart monitor, "we're losing her."

"Is everything okay?" My aunt's voice sounded very far away. I felt myself getting colder and smaller, like I was disappearing into the hard metal operating table. I did not try to move or speak and was not sure I could do either if I wanted to.

"It's a vagal reaction." The doctor was the only calm person in the room. She loaded a large needle with adrenaline and shot it into the IV. "This happens sometimes. It's okay."

They kept me lying down in the recovery room for a long time. The doctor came to check on me. She patted my hand. "Do you have any children?" I asked her. Tears leaked out of the corners of my eyes and soaked the sheets. Embarrassed, I tried to stop crying. When she told me she had a five-year-old son, I started sobbing all over again. I felt then that I had lost the only baby I would ever be lucky enough to have. Though no one had revealed the gender of the fetus, I knew it had to be a boy. I imagined he had curly brown hair and freckles and brown eyes, like Max.

For weeks afterward I did not leave the apartment. Once I finally did, I felt numb and empty as I made the motions of going to classes. I saw babies and pictures of babies everywhere—on the bus, in my professors' offices, at the park. Their innocent faces reproached me. I had done an unspeakable wrong. I felt sure that I had ruined any chance I had of having a family of my own.

Although fall had always been my favorite season, every year on the third Friday of October, a sadness would weigh on me. As the years passed, sometimes I would forget why I felt so bereft as the air turned crisp with the approach of winter. But never for long. I was mourning the death of my unborn son.

The third week of October 2003, at three o'clock in the morning, I was on all fours, my arms braced against our bed, with James, my midwife Megan, and Kathleen, my doctor who was there as a friend, all huddled at my backside.

"The baby's crowning," muttered Kathleen. I clawed the bed and straightened my legs, which were sore from squatting. "Where are you going, Jennifer?" Kathleen sounded worried. "Um, Jennifer? The baby's coming right now." Somewhere below me I heard Megan, who had birthed all ten of her children at home (five with the assistance of only her husband and her family), giggle good-naturedly.

"You're not going to drop it, are you?" I cried, putting my hand between my legs and feeling a hard head there. I didn't know why James, Megan, and Kathleen all laughed when I said that. I kept trying to get on the bed.

"Um, Jennifer?" Kathleen said again. "Now's not a really good time to change positions."

In one tremendous push, the baby burst from me. I managed to crawl onto the bed, and I twisted myself onto my back to see it.

"It's a boy," James said softly, his voice tender and amazed.

"No." I honestly did not believe him. After mistaking our first daughter, Hesperus, for a boy, I had gone on to have a second baby girl nineteen months later. Since I had grown up with no sisters, I was glad to have two daughters, and when I became pregnant again, I welcomed the idea of a third. Having a boy did not seem possible to me: After choosing to abort a fetus that I was sure had been a boy, I felt I had rendered my body incapable of growing and nurturing a son.

"Yes," James said in that same soft voice. "It's a boy."

"Is he okay?" The baby was so calm and wide-eyed and still. "Is he alive?" Kathleen rubbed him with a towel as he inched his way up my chest.

"He's perfect," Megan murmured. "He's just fine."

It took us more than two weeks to name our baby. During that time, he was very patient with us. Instead of crying, he made squeaky catlike noises. No matter how urgently he wanted to nurse, he stopped fussing the moment he saw my breast, gave a little guffaw or chuckle of pleasure, and then latched on. He was so sweet and affectionate and kind that I burst out crying one night.

"I don't deserve such a good baby," I sobbed to James. "I'm worried that I'll let him down. It isn't fair to him to have to have me as a mother. What if I don't do a good job?" James held me and let me cry.

"This is how you jump, Baby," explained two-and-a-half-year-old Athena, who refused to leave his side. She stayed by his bassinette as he slept, reading and singing to him and showing him, over and over, how to leap from the bed to the floor. I finally lured her away from her constant watch over him with the idea of baking our new baby a chocolate birthday cake and promised her his piece. "I love him more than all my stuffies," Hesperus confessed as the three of us, the three girls, tromped down to the kitchen. James joined us as we put half a candle in the cake and sang "Happy Birthday to Baby" loudly and off-key as he slept upstairs. We added a few extra verses to the song—"Happy Almost Half Birthday to Hesperus" and "Happy Almost Birthday to Athena"—and ate up the entire cake.

And finally, we named him: Etani Autumn. Etani means "my strength" in Hebrew; and his second name, Autumn, was in honor of the season. The day he was born, we had all walked together through the New England woods by our house, the leaves under our feet ablaze in the colors of the fall. The sorrow of autumn had become my strength. The suffocating sadness that came upon me each fall did not come that year.

I was ready, finally, to forgive myself.

Breaking the Curse

MARJORIE
OSTERHOUT

We thought the curse was real. And why wouldn't we? If anyone could bend fate to her will, it was my grandmother. She wore five earrings in each ear, sheared her hair in a near crewcut, and never, ever wore underwear. Angry, spiteful, and bitter, she once chased a robber from her house. Uphill. Waving a kitchen knife. Screaming. She stopped speaking to her sister for twenty years because of a spoon and wore black to my parents' wedding. As raving and lunatic as she could be, though, no one provoked more wrath from Nana than men. Any man. And we understood.

Her history with men was, without exception, terrible. During the Great Depression, her father forced her to leave home and make her own way, even though she was only a teenager. Her four husbands were unemployed, hard-drinking, and neglectful, which left her struggling as a single mother through World War II. When the fourth husband left, she named her dog after him and cursed her lineage. No boys would be born to her family. Ever.

The curse got off to a good start. My grandmother had daughters. Her daughters had daughters. Her granddaughters had daughters. Our family was made up of four generations of girls, nineteen in a row. As girl after girl was born, we stopped even thinking about boys. We just put the little pink dresses in boxes for the next baby girl, hung flowery wallpaper in all the bedrooms, and learned to chop wood and mow the lawn. So when I myself got pregnant, I figured I wouldn't need baby clothes. I didn't need crib sheets or receiving blankets. And I sure as heck didn't need advice. As the oldest of six sisters, I spent plenty of time changing diapers, explaining menstruation, and sharing eye shadow. Did I want a boy or a girl? It wasn't even a question. I had a pink baby shower and decided to name the baby Emma Lee.

Only one teensy problem presented itself: Emma Lee had a penis. There it was, on the ultrasound, a proud third leg pointing straight up. At first I was amused. Silly ultrasound! So much for modern technology! When the ultrasound technician assured me that the third leg was, indeed, a penis and not a wayward arm, I smiled indulgently. She didn't scare me with her 98 percent–positive-it's-a-boy speech. Give me the 2 percent! My family was all about beating the odds.

On to the amniocentesis. I didn't want it—nothing would stop me from having this baby—but my husband insisted, having worked with severely disabled children. It would help us prepare, he said, in case of the unexpected. Waiting for the results of the test was the most difficult two weeks of my pregnancy. In the end, chromosome 21 was normal, a nice matched pair with no sign of Down's syndrome. Chromosome 23, however, had an unexpected appearance: an X chromosome . . . and a Y chromosome.

Well. You can't argue with 100 percent. I was horrified, then grief stricken. Bye-bye makeup, giggling, and heart-to-heart talks. Hello wet dreams, whiskers, and underdressed girlfriends. Bye-bye to the daughter who would always be part of my life, who would send me thoughtful Mother's Day gifts and take care of me in my old age. Hello to the son who would disappear into his wife's family, forget my birthday, and stick me in the nursing home at the first creak.

It's not so much that I *wanted* a girl, or that I *didn't* want a boy. But I had *assumed* I was having a girl. Through my entire life I had never imagined anything different. I would have daughters, I would raise them to be strong and smart and unafraid, and then they would grow up to have babies and I would have granddaughters. Of *course* my baby was a girl. But she wasn't.

My husband tried to reassure me. I wouldn't be outnumbered—I would be special. Puberty talks would fall under his umbrella instead of mine. And I would dance with my son at his wedding. But beneath his reassurances, my husband was also surprised. He knew from day one that my family was estrogen central, that he probably wouldn't have a son to carry on his family name. He had met most of the nineteen girls. He had also met my grandmother before she died, and though she was relatively mellow in her old age, he recognized a force of nature when he saw one. Having daughters was practically written into our wedding vows.

That's when the bad dreams started. Most pregnant women have nightmares of the *Rosemary's Baby* type—giving birth to a monster, or losing the baby. But I dreamt about my grandmother. Although Nana had died ten years earlier, I was superstitious enough to believe she still had power over us. I kept dreaming about her holding a kitchen knife, glaring at me, refusing to speak to me. Adding to my fears were the many years of infertility that had preceded this pregnancy for me. According to the medical professionals, I wasn't supposed to be able to get pregnant, or to stay pregnant. But somehow I had. What if this baby—this boy—wasn't meant to be?

As it turns out, some forces of nature are stronger than others. My pregnancy went beautifully, without even a blip of morning sickness. Riding a happy hormone wave, I felt stronger and healthier than I ever had. I floated like a giant Macy's balloon, growing larger and larger. But I was tethered by fear. So much could go wrong, and I was afraid of falling in love with a baby I wasn't supposed to have.

I went into labor on my due date, and twenty-three hours later my son appeared. It was only then, groggy and exhausted, holding a healthy baby boy, that I began to believe he might be okay. Maybe we would be okay. Maybe I had a son.

For the first time, I thought about his name. Although I'd often imagined a daughter named Amy or Joy or Emma, I had never thought about boys' names. Even when that Y chromosome made its appearance, we were too afraid to choose a boy's name. So, for five days, I held Baby Boy Osterhout and pondered. I'd heard about babies who were born and just looked like an Abigail or a Henry, or babies who earned their names because they were born resembling their Grampa Charles or Aunt Kathy. But my baby didn't look like any name or person I could think of, and I was too tired and astonished by the pain of nursing to decide. Plus, what if I picked a name my grandmother hated? So his father named him. With a Dutch last name, he wanted a Dutch first name that was easy to spell and not too weird. Not Pim or Willem or Henk. And definitely not Teunis.

Ben.

A couple of months went by before I could relax into motherhood. Ben's early bout with jaundice and trouble nursing kept me metaphorically looking over my shoulder, and I continued to dream about my grandmother with her kitchen knife. The turning point came on Father's Day, when Ben let loose with his first smile. No tentative little grin, it was a real fireworks smile, huge and exuberant and . . . my grandmother's. I was speechless. Nana wasn't hovering on the edge of my dreams, threatening us from Beyond. She was here, part of Ben, inside him. I had misinterpreted my dream: She wasn't angry with me, and she wasn't threatening my boy. She was protecting us, standing guard with her kitchen knife, ready to chase another thief. She was on our side.

Ben is five now, and there's no doubt he has a Y chromosome. His first word was "truck." His second word was "bus." He is all about robots and machines. He's obsessed with fire trucks and loves to demonstrate his ability to pee standing up.

There's also no doubt about his lineage. He still has his grandmother's smile, though I see it far more often on him than I did on her. Like my grandmother, he is fiercely protective and determined to get what he wants. Unlike her, he doesn't seem to mind wearing underwear, and I hope I never see him with five earrings in each ear. But he's also inherited her softer traits: He's kind to animals, loves snow, and has a great belly laugh.

Will Ben have his own sons? Or is his Y chromosome a fluke? Only time will tell. But even if the curse holds, there is no doubt in my mind that I myself have been blessed.

WILL BOYS BE BOYS?

The Bully's Mother

KAREN E.
BENDER

Now he is six years old and a model citizen. He comes home and shows me the "Behavior Management" chart stapled to his kindergarten homework folder: For eighty-two of the last eighty-three days of school, he has received the esteemed mark of "personal best." He tells me that he and Jeff, his good friend, were the only ones in his class who were such good listeners that they were allowed to watch an ancient tape of *Casper the Friendly Ghost* in the classroom; the rest of his class was sentenced to the cafeteria to have a "quiet snack." He has been known to carry a potato bug carefully out of the house to set it on a flower outside. He sometimes asks his two-year-old sister, "Would you like to hold hands with me?" She nods vigorously, with her whole body, and he takes her hand and guides her down the sidewalk.

"He is just a sweetheart," says his teacher.

"He's a doll-baby," says another.

"He's so good," says a mother.

"Well," I say.

They are so reductive, these words: I am glad for them, but I do not want him to be caged by them. Then again, I do not want him to have the label that he wore four years ago. Then, when he was two and a half, I was the mother of the tiniest bully in the New York City preschools. He had the visage of an angel, the beautiful, trilling laugh of a forest creature. But for a year, he was the hitter, the pusher, and the biter of his preschool class.

My husband and I tend to think of ourselves as peaceful people. Of course, we have our moments, but by "peaceful" I mean that we are against war, fistfights, screaming matches in public places. My own childhood was shaped by my parents' desire for me to "be nice": My parents had been frightened by violent impulses expressed within their own families (my grandfather in South Dakota claimed that whenever a coworker on the railroad called him something anti-Semitic, "I hit him!"; my grandmother once allegedly threw a glass vase at my mother's older sister); and their solution was to train their girls to be restrained. The classic story in my family was that when I was two and a half and my sister was born, my parents bought me a Bozo-the-clown doll to punch whenever I wanted to hit her. Perhaps I sensed their wish for me to be a peacemaker: Instead of thrashing Bozo, I married him in a small ceremony in our backyard.

I was raised to feel somewhat proud of the fact that I was not one of the victimizers at my elementary school: I was, in some unfortunate moments, the victim. I was tiny, good at school, and bad at the sports that were valued in my Southern California elementary school in the 1970s. I remember walking around the school playground wishing I could trade my reading ability for the one to sock a rubber ball over a fence. My parents gave me lame responses to tell the girls who called me "Shrimpo" or "Small Fry." "Good things come in small packages" or "Bigger isn't better" just didn't cut it. "Shut up" might have, but I was not supposed to say these words at home; there was no way I could say them at school.

I dreamed of being a bully. I had dreams of pummeling rude girls with my fists until they screamed and ran from me. "Just shut up! You idiot!" I screamed at them, my body trembling. I woke up satisfied, and I was disoriented over my breakfast cereal. Who could I fight? What would it feel like to really hit someone, to feel their flesh under my outstretched hand? Would that quell the restlessness inside me?

I never found out.

Flash forward thirty years, past the thousands of insults, large and small, that make up civilized life. There were hundreds of arguments, some reasonable, some screamed; there were angry letters and emails, some sent and some not. I went through phases in which I was hyperdirect and sometimes insensitive; I went through avoidance periods; I pretended I was the type who let conflict slide off my skin. Some approaches worked, some didn't; and learning to assert myself in a way that felt easy and true remained a struggle.

When our son was born, my husband and I saw him as the purest being in the world, all impulses raw and new, untainted by other people. We did not want to wreck him, we did not want to repress him; we wanted him to have access to all of himself to help him negotiate a difficult world. In the year of his infancy, I watched other children in the sandbox and felt the discomfort that many new mothers have at the shouting, the grabbing, the violence shimmering under these babyish faces. Why were so many kids grabbing toys from each other? When my son was old enough to play like that, would other kids grab from him, too? And if they did—what would he do?

Jonah's first playdates, when he was one, were peaceful operations, in which the kids scrounged around each other's toys and ignored each other. When the children turned two, my friends, who were also older, first-time mothers, were shocked by the depths of greed that existed in our boys, the compulsive need for any toy anyone else was holding. We had imagined, idiotically, that if we treated our babies with painstaking thoughtfulness and gentleness, they would be, well, nicer. "Oh my goodness!" one mother said, as her son grabbed a truck from another boy and both children rolled on the floor, wailing. The playdates always ended abruptly, with many apologies.

We had no idea what lay ahead.

The first time Jonah bit someone, it was me. I don't remember the exact situation—he was two, I was carrying him somewhere, he was throwing a fit, and he bit me. It was a small nip, it did not break the skin, and it puzzled me more than anything else. That was, looking back, the moment I should have done it, said a strong *no*, given him a time-out, done whatever the correct, final thing might have been that would have effectively stopped it.

But I was more focused on trying to understand him, the way I felt I had not been understood as a child. "I know you're mad," I murmured. "It's hard. I know."

I did not say "No" when he bit me that first time.

The next time he tried it, I ducked.

He did not discover his teeth as a weapon against other children until he was squabbling over a toy with his best friend, Matt. They both were clinging to a large plastic car. Matt's mother and I were having the speedy, frantic conversation of mothers who try to cram a day's worth of adult discussion into twenty minutes, and the boys were grunting at each other. I saw Jonah give me an anguished glance. "Hold on," I told him—my next mistake. For then there was a scream.

Jonah took off with the car. Matt fell to the floor, then ran weeping to his mother, holding out his hand.

"He bit him!" said Matt's mother. "Jonah bit him."

"What?" I said, pathetically. I looked and saw the curved indentation of Jonah's teeth on Matt's hand. My heart began pounding. "Oh, no."

I stood there burning with shame, a hot, constricting coat I wanted to shrug off. "I'm sorry," I said. I could not believe it: My son had injured another child. I bent down and looked into my child's guileless face. "No," I said, carefully, to my son. "Don't do that. No."

I stood up again, unsure how to inhabit my new role as the bully's mother. Should I apologize for my son? Should I offer Matt an icepack? Should I help him clean the wound? I was motionless, useless, trying to beat back the thought: I was glad that Jonah was not the injured one.

"Tell him sorry!" said Matt's mother to Jonah.

"Tell him sorry," I said to Jonah, who ducked under a chair and laughed.

What do you do when someone bumps into you on the subway? What do you do when someone you love leaves you, when someone dumber than you gets the job you want, when your landlord decides to kick you out of your apartment and then sleeps even more peacefully at night? Here was Jonah, inducted into the world of disappointment, frustration, other people's aggravating needs. Here was my son, not wanting to share. He was dealing with it by biting, and I did not know what to do.

Did it matter that he was a boy? Some experts explain biting as a frustration response when language has not been developed: That might explain the proliferation of boy biters, as their language is slower to develop. But a happy, controlled kind of violence tended to be part of my son's playdates, even the friendly ones. In fact, after the biting incident with Matt, controlled violence was what we aimed for: plastic swords hitting trees, not hands; cars crashing into sidewalks, not feet. Jonah and his friends could not pick up a stick without making it into a weapon; my husband said they would not go out unless fully armed.

The controlled violence fascinated me: It seemed that my son had access to an aggression that I never had. Was this clear channel that boys had to their own aggression what had helped them, over the centuries, gain so much power? Should I try to learn from the giddy way they slammed swords into couches, pummeled trees? I did not want to interfere with this part of my son, the part that bit into the world with a heady excitement, that did not want to please or accommodate but wanted just to *get*. What would happen if I did not interfere with this impulse in him?

I did watch him, nervously, during these playdates, ready to tackle both parties if he and another child had their hands on the same toy. There was one more bite, in the sandbox—no blood, but a ruckus nonetheless—and after this one I yelled, despairingly, at him in the stroller: "You. Must. Not. Bite." He gazed beyond me, uninterested in my nattering.

When he started preschool a few months later, I furtively watched the other children in his class and wondered what secrets their parents held. My son looked innocent, and I wanted to coast on that, at least briefly. I did not tell the teacher he had bitten before—I did not want to stigmatize him, and besides, under my hawklike watch, he had not perpetrated any recent incidents.

"Have a good time," I said, kissing him, and I left.

All was well for the first few months of school. After I dropped him off each day, my control over Jonah's behavior consisted of thinking obsessively, "Don't hurt anyone. Don't hurt anyone. Please." Then one day I went to pick him up, and the security gate swung open to Peter, the twenty-something childcare teacher with the gigantic blue eyes of a Madame Alexander doll. He did not look happy to see me. "Andrea wants to speak with you," he said. A path was cleared for me to speak with Andrea, the senior teacher, who looked as regal and solemn as she could while perched on a kid-sized plastic chair.

"Is everything all right at home?" she asked, looking at me.

What kind of question was this? What qualified as all right? "Uh, I think so," I said.

"Anything different over the weekend?" she continued.

"My husband was out of town for a couple days," I said.

She paused. Then she said, carefully, "Will he be back?"

My hands began to shake. "He's already back," I said. Feeling the need to explain, I went on: "He was at a job interview. I mean, he has a job. At the moment. This is a better job. Not that the current job is not fine—"

"I wanted to know," she said, "because Jonah bit Lily today."

I felt my heart jump. "What did she do?" I asked.

"Violence is never the answer," said Andrea, trying not to look aghast.

I was supposed to be playing a different role. I was supposed to be humble, apologetic, concerned. I was those things, deeply, plus ashamed. But I also wanted to know what little Lily had done. Did she grab a toy? Did she step on him? Why did he do this?

"Of course," I said, gritting my teeth, "but what exactly was happening—"

"They were sitting next to each other while they had snack," Andrea began, "and Jonah spilled a little juice out of his cup. Lily, who is"— she shrugged here—"boisterous, yelled, 'No!' in a loud voice. And then Jonah," she said, her voice hardening, "bit her."

There was a different tone in Andrea's voice when she described little Lily's outburst and Jonah's biting. Why was Lily "boisterous" and Jonah a villain? Why was she seeing Jonah as a tormentor, an out-of-control child, while darling Lily, the vulnerable girl, was merely boisterously innocent?

"I'm sorry," I said.

"We have to tell him that it is not acceptable," said Andrea, and then my boy fell into my arms.

One friend suggested that Jonah wear a bagel on a string around his neck, reasoning that if he felt like biting someone, he could bite that. One mother read me a passage in a dumb psychology book that suggested I bite my son ("gently") on the finger to show him "how it felt." Lily's mother walked by me on the street and refused to look at me. I would kiss my son before I left him at school and whisper, "Remember. No biting. No hitting. Use words." I began to dread the walk to the preschool when I went to pick him up, waiting for Andrea to tell me there had been "another incident." Sometimes when mothers learned who my son was, they said, "Oh, *you're* Jonah's mom," as though they knew something about me that I did not. There was, I found, a special shame to being allied with the victimizer. The victims were hugged, coddled, given treats. The victimizer was shunned. I felt a new sympathy for criminals. Shame was terrible, the feeling of not quite being human, due to actions that were actually quite human indeed, albeit totally out of control.

We tried. We tried the stick theory. We gave him time-outs. We withheld videos. He did not receive the precious balloon he wanted on the walk home from school. We coached him with alternative strategies: Instead of hitting someone, say, "I need space!" we said, to which he responded by hitting a classmate and then yelling, "I need space!" We tried the carrot approach: If he made it six weeks without hurting anyone, he would receive a new garbage truck.

Somehow, when we acted quickly and consistently, giving him a punishment the moment he bit or hit, he got it: The biting stopped. He learned how to arm himself with a loud "No!" or "Stop it!" or "That's mine!" I didn't quite believe the behavior was gone; I still approached the doors of the school with fear. The biting had created an almost primitive fury in the other parents: It was as though they realized how quickly children could become feral. But somehow, it stopped.

"He hit Ben," Jonah's teacher, Peter, reported one day.

"He didn't bite him, though?" I asked, hopefully.

"No," said Peter.

I viewed this as progress. But hitting was still forbidden at the preschool, and one day, when I picked up Jonah, Peter said brightly, "Jonah hit Zack and so the class got together and yelled at him, 'No hitting!'"

"They did what?" I asked.

Jonah cried the rest of the afternoon. I held him, trying to comfort him, ashamed that we had not been able to prevent this, that it took a posse of two-year-olds to intervene. But then he stopped hitting, too. Gradually, the ice that lodged in my throat when I went to school pickup disappeared. Andrea and Peter were more welcoming. "He had a great day," chirped Andrea one morning; "He always has great days." I stared at her; had she already forgotten? But they, as preschool teachers, understood something that mothers gradually learn: that children evolve in phases. I had not seen any way out of it, but they had known that, with effort, this would also pass.

Jonah became four, then five, and now he is six. Now he is scornful of the children in his class who have not learned the social skills that he has. "Did you know that Carl lost all of his privileges because he pushed Ned?" he said. "Now that is really sad." But he is still figuring it out, as we all are, the pas de deux that is not just a boy or a girl problem—the endless dance everyone does with their own aggressiveness, trying to figure out how to honor their own feelings, understand other people's, and express themselves so that we can all get along.

One morning, we were all sitting around the breakfast table. "John said he was smarter than me," he told us suddenly, his brow furrowed.

"That is just ridiculous," I said.

My husband opened his arms. "Do you know how much I love you?" my husband said, hugging him tightly.

But while Jonah accepted a hug, he stirred his cereal around with his spoon unhappily. He did not know how to respond to this.

"If he says it again, do you know what to say?" I said.

"What?" he asked.

"Say, 'You're a fool,'" I said.

Was this the right response? I didn't know.

My son looked at me. And then he laughed.

Will Boys Be Boys?

ROCHELLE
SHAPIRO

My ideas about raising a son were born under the buzz of fluorescent lights. It was in a basement where I met with my consciousness-raising group in the early seventies. We were feminists. We lamented our imposed limitations—our cluelessness in math and science, our deference to men, our dependency, and our fear of success. But we didn't blame men. We felt for them—always measuring themselves by how much money they made; their bellicose toys that led to war; their restlessness except if they were watching sports on TV; the way they couldn't show their feelings, weren't allowed to cry.

"When we have sons," our leader said, forcefully, "we aren't going to let them fall into gender traps." She had a no-nonsense look—jeans, a black t-shirt, and very short hair. "We'll let them grow their hair long," she said, "and wear pink and let them take ballet lessons with their sisters and let them learn to cook. Dolls are good for teaching boys parenting skills. Buy them dolls. And above all, boys have to be allowed to cry." We all applauded.

When my son was born, he seemed to have learned the lesson in utero that men don't cry. If he was hungry or colicky, he uttered a few "eh, eh, eh"s with maybe a tremble of the lips, and that was it. When he was about six months old, as I held him, his face turned a purple red, his body became rigid, his mouth opened, but he didn't cry. I was terrified. I thought he was dying of SIDS, but then I noticed that his two-and-a-half-year-old sister was biting his hand.

I tried to get him unisex socialized so he could develop his gentleness. Of course, I bought him a football and a Wiffle ball with a plastic bat and a little spongy basketball with a hoop that attached to his bedroom door, but I also encouraged my husband to cook with him, and I enrolled my son in the same pre-ballet class that my daughter was taking. Instead of dancing, my son spent the class swinging from the ballet barre and running around the room, waving at himself in the big mirror. I dressed my son in blue, but I also bought him pink t-shirts for under his striped OshKosh overalls. I tried to let his blond curls grow, but I'd find them on the bathroom carpet: He'd snipped them off in protest with his sister's blunt arts-and-crafts scissors.

"I'm a boy," he said as if he needed to set it straight with me.

I had to admit he was different from his sister. She used to love sitting in her carriage, being wheeled through the streets, but even with the safety harness zipped on, my son would vault himself over the side and dangle there like a trapeze artist. If he spotted a cement mixer or a sanitation truck or a fire engine, he was transfixed. He could spend ages turning the handle of a can opener to watch the gear move or taking apart an old radio or opening and closing the shower door to see how it slid on the runner.

In toy stores, he insisted on Matchbox cars that he would carry around in his pockets. He baby talked his father into buying him little plastic soldiers. With the green plastic boxes that strawberries used to come in, he'd build tall battlements and hitch the soldiers onto them. Even though I never exposed my children to the graphic images on the news or let them watch violent shows, a whole afternoon could pass with him making sounds of bullets whizzing through the air and strangled noises emulating the deaths of plastic soldiers. For balance, I bought him a small boy doll that had blond curls and big brown eyes like he did.

"You can be his daddy," I told him.

When he carried it upstairs, I imagined him playing father with it, rocking the doll in his small arms or tucking it into his bed with whatever lines he could recite from Margaret Wise Brown's *Good Night Moon*, which I used to read to him. Within the hour, I noticed a water stain spreading on the ceiling of my den. I rushed upstairs and found a geyser shooting from the toilet and flooding the bathroom floor. My son, over his baby shoes in water, was trying to mop it up with my bathrobe.

"How did this happen?" I asked him.

He just shrugged.

I turned off the water valve and called the plumber, who snaked the toilet; like a birth, out came the little blond head, then the shoulders, and then the whole wet baby doll.

Despite my feminist efforts, my son was determinedly a traditional boy. The love of wrestling seemed to be encoded into his DNA. Without ever having come into contact with a wrestler, while my husband was lying on the carpet, watching TV, my son would leap on him and try to get him into a headlock. And my son was strong and fearless. He shinnied up telephone poles. One winter day, when I couldn't find him, our upstairs neighbor phoned to say that he saw him out his window on the highest limb of an elm, like a sparrow bundled in a snowsuit. The fire department had to get my son down.

When he was four, he would bend his knees, wrap his arms around his big sister's legs, and stand up, lifting her off the floor even though she had a good fifteen pounds on him. She began to call him Bam Bam, after the stone age powerhouse kid on the Flintstones. We hadn't worried that he'd have trouble with playground bullies, but someone was always knocking him over, pushing him off the slide, or throwing sand in his eyes in the sandbox.

Before I could get off the bench to intercede, his sister, always very tall for her age, would go over to the bully and declare, "This is my brother. And I'm this big." She would put the flat of her hand at the top of her head. "And you're only this big," and she'd lower her hand to the trembling kid's head. "Get it?" she would ask, and the bully always got it.

What a contradiction! Although my daughter was tall, she was narrow with delicate wrists and ankles, and she had a china doll face. My son was sturdy, broad-shouldered, with wide hands, but couldn't stand up to aggression.

When he began kindergarten, there was a nasty kid, Adam, who threw my son's lunch out the bus window, stuck gum in his hair, and tripped him. If I called Adam's parents or went to the teacher, Adam would get other kids to taunt my son. Every day, my son came off the school bus with a knob on his head or a scratch on his face. I began to regret all those pink t-shirts, the ballet classes, the cooking, the whole consciousness-raising group.

One day, when he got off the school bus, his face was red and trembling. I didn't ask him what happened right away because he looked close to tears, and for him, it would be the worst thing to cry in front of the other children.

When we got home, I bent down, put my hand on his shoulder, and looked into his eyes. "Are you all right?" I asked.

For the first time, he began to sob loudly, tears streaming down his face. Finally, he gasped, "I hit Adam back."

I was as choked up as he was. He hadn't been afraid to stand up to a bully. He knew how strong he was. But he was a pacifist, a brave turn-the-other-cheeker.

"I know you wouldn't have hit him unless you had no choice," I said.

He nodded gravely and swiped his tears with the back of his hand.

My son was a sensitive soul after all, sensitive and deep, macho and gentle. How had I missed this? I was too busy promoting a philosophy to notice.

After that, I never tried to guide him to be anyone other than who he already was. When he wanted to wrestle, I cheered in the bleachers. If he didn't cry during a sad movie, I minded my own business. He's neither all macho nor all sensitive, neither New Age male nor traditionalist. What he is is a person in his own right, worthy of celebration.

Zen and the Art of Extracurricular Activities

GAYLE
BRANDEIS

My son has always been into bows and arrows, or "bare and orrows," as he used to call them. I am not sure when exactly the fascination began, but it quickly hit the bull's eye of his young male heart.

When Arin was three, he fashioned a bow and arrow out of a curved stick and a piece of string and gleefully shot sticks into the distance. For his fourth birthday, we threw him a Robin Hood–themed party at a park. The kids in attendance made Robin Hood hats out of newspaper, searched for gold coins (the chocolate oozing from the foil in the midday sun), and ate copious amounts of cake (covered with tiny knights—the closest thing we could find to Robin Hood). The pièce de résistance, for Arin at least, was when the kids lined up and took turns shooting plastic suction-cupped arrows from a limp-stringed, 99 cent store–bought bow at a target I had chalked onto a rickety green easel.

Even as a passionate antiweapon pacifist, I somehow had no problem with Arin's bows and arrows. Other than a target, Arin never actually shot his arrows at anything, or, more importantly, anyone. Plus, archery held quasi-romantic associations for me—stealing from the rich, giving to the poor, etc., etc.

I had read *Zen in the Art of Archery* in college, and anything related to Zen carried with it a kind of beatific, crystalline glow for me. So, when I discovered that there was an archery school in our town, Arin and I were both excited about it. Arin was the perfect age—seven, the age that kids are eligible for the Junior Olympic Archery League. I signed him up for his first lesson on Valentine's Day. I pictured him as a cupid with love-tipped arrows, practicing with serene concentration in a dojo-like environment—pure, clean, lots of silence and light.

When we arrived at the school, located in an industrial complex in a remote part of town, I began to realize that I had probably idealized the experience, as I am wont to do. When we opened the door, I knew this was indeed the case. Somewhere, in my Buddhist revolutionary fantasies, I had completely overlooked the fact that people use bows and arrows to kill things. Lots of things. Lots of beautiful things. The walls of the professional shop and the archery range were covered with "trophies"—six sweet-faced deer chopped off at the necks, a couple of bighorn sheep, an entire mounted bobcat, and three wild boars (one of which was set up in an elaborate tableaux, half of its body jutting out of a fake cave on the wall). In the shop, you could buy "realistic animal targets," which at first glance seemed to be glossy door-sized photo posters of deer, bear, elk, and other gorgeous animals. Upon closer examination, I noticed lines drawn on the animal images, almost like those on a butcher's chart, to indicate how to aim your arrow closest to the animal's pulpy, red heart. Above all, this scene rattled my vegetarian sensibilities.

Arin, my omnivorous son, didn't seem perturbed in the least, although his eyes were clearly fixated on all the "bare and orrows" in the room and not the things they killed. Strangely, in the midst of all these targets and specialty wrist guards and the other assorted hunting gear, there was a glass display case stuffed to the brim with cheerful, colorful, Beanie Babies. And next to the spinning racks of hunting videos was a corner stocked with dingy baby toys, where my then four-year-old daughter, Hannah, halfheartedly played during Arin's lesson.

Far from the white-clad, monklike clientele I had envisioned, the archery studio was filled with beer-bellied, dirty jeans–clad, bearded men, and curiously tall, pale, haunted-looking children with stringy hair. The lesson itself was decidedly un-Zenlike as well. The instructor told Arin to "let go" at one point, but he was talking about the string of the bow, not the trappings of Arin's seven-year-old ego. Arin, nervous and excited to the point of catatonia at the beginning of the lesson, was so comfortable by the end that he actually shot an arrow into the yolk-yellow center of the target. I have to admit, I did have a little tingle of a thrill watching him in his Robin Hood stance, even if it was decidedly un-Cupidlike.

Arin was totally jazzed on the way home. He said that he wanted to come back every Saturday, but I didn't know if I could stand to experience looking into all those glassy animal eyes on the wall again. I didn't know if I wanted my son to hang around with a bunch of people who killed animals for fun. I didn't know how much my personal politics and passions should influence his desires.

Back at home, I dusted off my dog-eared and note-filled copy of *Zen in the Art of Archery*. I closed my eyes, opened it randomly, and pointed. Whatever phrase my finger landed on, I told myself, would reveal what I needed to know.

I ended up with the following "advice": "Bow[s] and arrow[s] are only a pretext for something that could just as well happen without them, only the way to the goal, not the goal itself, only helps for the last decisive leap." Despite the ambiguity of the message, and the likelihood that I would take to heart only that which served me, I decided to take a decisive leap of my own. Bows and arrows are not the only way to the goal, so the passage read. I contacted the local soccer league and signed Arin up—an activity I sensed we could both live with.

Arin is fourteen now. He is still interested in "bare and orrows," but he has found another violent pastime to obsess about—paintball. Many of his friends have all the paintball gear—the guns (or "markers," as the ads call them), the helmets, the chest protectors. They have their own little battles in the river bottom near our house, and they come home covered with splotches of neon pink and blue. On occasion Arin has joined in the shenanigans, something that drives me out of my pacifist mind. I just can't seem to reconcile the fact that I participate in weekly antiwar protests and my son (a professed pacifist himself) is lusting to play war games. He wants a paintball gun more than anything else in the world. It's what he's saving his money for (although I haven't given him the okay to purchase anything at this point. It's all theoretical right now; his savings have dwindled down to about ten dollars, so it will be a while before he can even afford "ammunition").

We have been dancing around each other over the issue, and once again I'm faced with the question—how much should I let my own personal politics influence and limit my son's passions? I haven't come to a firm decision yet. Part of me wants to say, No, No, No—I want nothing related to weapons in this house at all. Another part wants to give my son the freedom to explore his own interests, even if they don't jive with my ideals. Maybe if kids play war games, they'll get all that violent juice out of their systems and will release the need to actually go to war someday. I don't know.

I recently attended the Mama Gathering in L.A., a conference for radical mothers. Before the first workshop started, I found myself speaking with a woman who was going to be teaching a session on peaceful parenting. She asked if I had brought my kids with me to the event; I shook my head and asked if she had, herself.

"No," she said. "My son's off paintballing."

"How do you feel about that?"

She sighed and smiled. "I figure he needs to go in the opposite direction from me in order to find himself."

That night, a little achy from the radical cheerleading workshop ("There's room in our womb for revolution!"), I cracked open Zen in the Art of Archery again. I found this: "How far the pupil will go is not the concern of the teacher and master. Hardly has he shown him the right way when he must let him go on alone."

I know my son will one day fly away from me like an arrow from a bow. I know he is trying to shape himself into his own bow so he can launch himself in the direction of his choosing. I know I have tried to show him the right way (at least what I've considered to be the right way). Maybe that's all I can really do as a mom. I still haven't given him the okay to bring gunlike things into the house. But if he comes home one day dressed like a storm trooper and covered with gobs of color, of course I'll hug him. Even if it means I'll get stained with a little bit of paint, myself.

Full House

FAULKNER
FOX

"**I**t must be so much easier to have two of a kind," friends with a son and a daughter will sometimes say to me, "two boys who want to do the same things." And this is basically true, I suppose, of my sons and their largely self-ticking world of play. Except, of course, when Ben is in an outside mood while Joseph wants to be cozy inside, or Joseph wants to open the new game right away while Ben wants to save it, or Joseph doesn't want to do what Ben has suggested *because* Ben has suggested it.* It's not as if shared gender assures lack of conflict, after all.

Still, when I see my friend Sarah set her daughter, Chloe, up with macramé so she can pitch to her son, Roger, I think, *Jeez. Does life have to be so gendered? Can't they both macramé, then play ball together, leaving Sarah on the sidelines to read a magazine?*

I'm happy to say that I get to read some magazines now while on duty as the mother of seven- and ten-year-old boys. I view this state of affairs

---

* *I've changed the names of everyone in this piece to protect their privacy.*

as a triumph, pretty much, since I'm still retroactively tired from the more intensive mothering I did when they were younger. And I wonder how much of the ease I currently experience has to do with my sons' shared boyness.

Right now, Ben and Joseph are passionate about building castles, railroad tracks, and Lego vehicles; collecting baseball cards; playing baseball, poker, and Monopoly; and making their own strange action movies. In all of this, they are each other's favorite playmate, sometimes—but not always—negating the need for my participation. Sure, I play poker and catch with them, but I don't have to. They have each other. Usually I feel relieved by this. Sometimes I feel left out.

In the first six years of parenthood, I never felt left out. There was too much going on—and required. Despite Ben and Joseph's typical joy with each other and keen interest in the world of play, my husband, Duncan, and I felt overwhelmed at times, as people with young children often do. Certainly, our family and house felt full, chock-full. And then when Joseph was six and Ben three and a half, I got pregnant, unintentionally. What should we do? We hadn't planned this! I like to plan things. Before we could get used to the idea of the pregnancy, it became clear that I was likely to miscarry. I realized then that I really wanted this baby to live. I thought of it as a daughter more often than I thought of it as a son. Of course, I wasn't sure it was a daughter. Still, it might be. I miscarried at ten weeks, and it took me more than two years to be ready to hold a simple ending ceremony, marking the loss.

Soon after that ceremony, Duncan and I decided that we did want to have a third child, and that we would try for one, on purpose. We got pregnant, and I had a very early miscarriage. Two months later, I got pregnant again. That time I miscarried on the last day of the first trimester.

Why couldn't we leave well enough alone? We had a full house—we had the boys. They were curious, exuberant, loving, and joyful children. Certainly, our lives felt rich, busy, and full. Duncan often voiced concerns about the planet, about overpopulation. "We shouldn't do more than replace ourselves," he'd say. I could certainly see his point.

Now, though, we didn't just have two sons. We had three miscarriages on top of those sons. That's how it felt to me. I don't know who those children were, but I think of them as lost girls, in a way. The daughter I won't have. Friends who know about the miscarriages ask, kindly, if it makes me sad to see babies. It doesn't. But sometimes it makes me sad to see girls—of any age. Other people's daughters. I think of countries, like China, where daughters are not wanted, and I feel drawn there. Duncan isn't quite on board with this plan. So we haven't gone. Maybe we won't ever go.

I never wish that my sons were daughters. I love their son-ness. But sometimes I ask, just kiddingly, if I can paint their fingernails, if they want to have a tea party, if they'll play house with me. Mom, they say in fake exasperation, and then they laugh because they know I'm teasing. And then I tickle them, according to their one-word direction: "unstoppingly."

My brother, Justin, just had a second son. Two boys, two years and a few months apart—like my sons. "There's a curse on our family," Joseph said when he heard about his new cousin's gender. "No one can have girls!" Joseph is very melodramatic, he likes to overstate and stir up controversy.

"Boys are awesome," I say back. "It's not a curse to have boys."

"Do you ever wish you had a daughter?" Benjamin or Joseph will sometimes ask. "Yes," I say, "but I never wish you were a girl."

I started to want a third child, in earnest, during Joseph's first baseball season. The following spring, when Ben joined Joseph's league, my longing grew more acute. Perhaps this timing is a coincidence. It's also possible, though, that my desire was connected to the way I felt left out as my sons made their first foray into all-male sports. They were growing up, going somewhere I couldn't go with them. This thought may have stirred my longing for a third child, a child I consciously hoped, this time, would be a girl.

Baseball wasn't the gentle co-ed soccer Joseph and Ben had previously played. Some baseball dads yelled at the players. And some players cried, just like seven-, eight-, and nine-year-old boys do. When no one was crying or yelling in anger, it was great fun to be a Little League parent. I learned to keep the team's official score, and at home, I practiced catching, throwing, and hitting with my sons nearly every day. At the games, though, I was on the sidelines in a way I had never been before in their lives, and in a way that Duncan wasn't. Why this distinction? Was it simply because Duncan has a better throwing arm than I do? If so, why is his arm better? I played softball for two years, from age eight to ten, and I'm left-handed. Joseph loves to tell me, as a form of encouragement, that "all the great pitchers are left-handed." Why couldn't I throw as well as my husband? I called my father to find out.

"Did anyone ever teach me to throw like a boy?" I asked. "I'm wondering if I forgot, or if I never knew."

"No one taught you," my father said. "We didn't think it was important at the time."

This fact disturbed me. And yet I knew that throwing well hadn't been important to me at the time, either. The following year, I quit softball and became a cheerleader for a boys' football team instead. Cheerleading was an unfortunate, if exclusive, sideline sport that I participated in for the next five years.

I don't want to be sidelined in my sons' lives. Not that I expect to go everywhere, hand in hand, with them—on their first grown-up dates, for example. Here are some questions I often wonder about: If I had a daughter, would I be less left out as she grew up? What if she was really girly, way girlier than I am? Whatever her level of girliness, wouldn't she need her privacy? Wouldn't I need mine?

I'm not sure whether it's an overgeneralization or a truth that mothers and daughters are more intimate than any other constellation of parent and child. The possibility that it's true is part of what makes me long for a daughter. I imagine the bonding things we might do together, things I'm not even sure I enjoy that much, like painting each other's nails.

Just this past weekend, I was sitting on the bed, in my bathrobe, noticing—among other things—that my toenails were not at their best. Ben came up and wanted to Magic Marker them blue. I let him, and then he did his own to match. It was almost like painting, without the horrible smell. It was better than painting, in fact. And as we lay there chatting, him holding my foot and coloring intently, it was as intimate as intimate gets. He didn't need to be a girl, and I didn't need to throw better, in that moment. It was just us, together, mother and son.

It Takes a Village

JENNIFER
LAUCK

The front porch of our new house is the whole front of the house, and it's like the stern of a great ship. It's so high, I can look down and see my entire new neighborhood with its old houses and older trees. I can wave at our new neighbors. I can watch our new mail carrier approach with her letters and packages.

I haven't actually been out on this porch much. I had a baby two months ago and have been in the house, in a kind of lockdown, fulfilling the needs of a newborn. Spencer's days have been spent in school, and his afternoons have been inside with me, but it's spring break. It's also one of the first really nice days. Spencer was like a puppy, begging to be outside, and I let him go out, as long as he promised to stay in front of our house.

I put the baby down for a nap and came out on our porch to look for him.

Overhead, the sky is cloudy, but the clouds are high and pulled apart, and the street is covered with the petals of little white flowers that were blown off the trees by a fast spring shower.

"Spencer!" I yell.

"What?"

"Where are you?"

"In the garage!" he yells.

I'm holding the receiver of the baby monitor, my baby alert system, and it's turned up high enough to hear her breathing. I hook the receiver on my pants pocket and go down to the sidewalk.

Across the way, two older boys lean against a tree. I've seen them on the street, but I don't really know them.

I think the blond one is Robert and the dark-haired one is Frank, or maybe the blond is Frank and the dark-haired one is Robert.

I wave at them with new-neighbor enthusiasm.

"Hi, guys," I say.

The blond kid waves back, but the other one pretty much ignores me.

A tennis ball rolls out of the garage, and it's followed by another tennis ball, a basketball, and finally, a soccer ball with SPENCER written all over it in permanent black ink.

My boy is deep within the garage, bent over a bin of toys and tossing things out as fast as he can grab them.

"What are you doing?" I say.

"I'm looking for my sword."

I take a big step over broken hunks of sidewalk chalk, remotes for two battery-operated cars, and a baseball mitt.

"What sword?" I say.

"My Nerf sword," he says.

Spencer sounds a little peeved that I don't know what sword he's searching for, but I ignore his irritated tone and decide to do what I do best, which is the act of organizing any mess made by my child. I can't help it, putting things in order helps me think, and so I get busy while he continues his search.

"Spence," I say, "hand me that bucket in the corner."

"Mo-ooom," he says, "I need my sword."

"Bucket first," I say.

He grabs the bucket and drops it next to me with a bang.

"Thank you," I say.

I sort good chalk from bad chalk, making two little piles.

"Why do you need the sword?" I say.

"Because," he says.

"Because why?" I say.

"Because we're going to kill someone," Spencer says.

My hands continue to sort—good chalk, bad chalk, keep, toss—and it's my "do not react" mode that has come from years of training. See, Spencer's been on a killing or being killed death trip for about three years now. When he was about two, he picked up an empty paper towel roll, pointed at me like a marksman, and said, "Bang." Since then, he's escalated to war games and ninja battles. It's literally nonstop.

I've been pretty much on my own with this situation too. If my mother friends admit they have a boy like Spencer, most of them blow it off and say it's a "stage." The rest of them just shake their heads, bewildered, and tell me stories of how their boys are so peaceful and peace loving.

I try not to sound exasperated, even though I am.

"Please stop with the killing talk already," I say. "We don't kill anyone, and besides, those boys are too old for you and I need you to stay here, in front of the house."

Spencer gets all bendy at his knees, hands shaking like they are wet.

"But we *are* in front of the house," he says.

"They are across the street," I say. "You need to be on this side of the street."

Spencer lets go with a full-blown fit of tears, and it's the kind of scene that I hate as much as I hate the killing mode.

I stop with my organizing and get a paper towel from the shelf. I wipe his nose and look at him, trying to think what to do.

My mind chatter goes a little like this: *He wants to play but I don't know these kids but it's probably okay since they are from the street but they look a little shady but I'm probably being paranoid.*

What to do, what to do?

"Blow," I say.

Spencer honks into the paper towel and takes his fit down to a series of loud inhales and gulps.

I look from the boys to Spencer again (now giving me the pathetic puppy eyes).

"Come on," I say.

We go down the driveway to the curb. Little white flower petals move under our feet as we cross the street.

"Hey, guys," I say.

The kids nod but aren't overly chatty. I decide to build a little rapport.

"You're Robert, right?" I say. "And you're Frank?"

The boys nod and that's one point for me. I know them and they know I know them. I ask a couple more questions about the whereabouts of their mothers and their ages. Robert is six; his mom is at work but there is a baby sitter at his house. Frank is seven, and his mother is at his house, on the corner, and she trusts him to play on the street unsupervised.

I hold up Spencer's hand like we are a team.

"Spencer is five," I say, "and if you want to play with him, that's great, but he needs to be on our side of the street, okay?"

I smile like we can all be pals.

"And let's not kill anyone today, huh?" I say. "Why not have a pretend sword duel and just get a little cut instead?"

Robert smiles like this is perfectly acceptable to him, but now Frank is looking pretty bored. He actually rolls his eyes with the expertise of a fifteen-year-old.

"Okay, Frank?" I say.

Saying his name makes him look my way, and he gives a small nod that says that he hears me.

Spencer and I go back to our side of the street, but he tries to yank free of my hand while looking back at the two boys.

"Come on, guys," he says. "Come over and let's play."

When we get to our side of the street, I go into the garage. A couple minutes of searching nets the Nerf sword, and I take it to Spencer. He grabs it and waves it at the boys, but they ignore him.

The tip of his Nerf sword drops into the gutter.

"They aren't coming, Mom," he says.

"They will, Honey," I say, "or they won't but it's okay. You'll figure something out, or you can come into the house and we'll play with the baby."

"I don't want to be inside anymore," he says. "I want to play with kids."

Spencer watches the boys with a naked longing that only kids allow themselves to show, and it's enough to break my heart. Through the baby monitor, I can hear Jo's dove calls. I put my arm around Spencer's shoulders and try to convince him how being inside can be fun too, but he's just not interested.

"I have to go in and feed her now," I say. "You must stay here, in front of the house. Okay?"

Spencer whacks at the curb with his sword, sending the white flower petals into little frenzies of flight.

"Okay?" I say.

He looks over at the boys again, only they are walking up the steps to Robert's house. Spencer whacks at the curb again.

"Okay," he says.

Over the next thirty minutes, it's clear that Spencer isn't going to stay in front of the house. Twice, I come out to find him with Robert and Frank, down at the corner of our street and then around the corner. The third time, I call him in and arrange a playdate with a little boy down the street named Malcolm. Of course, I don't know Malcolm that well either, but I do know that he likes to be inside, drawing. What could be more harmless than that?

A couple hours later, Josephine is fed, changed, and alert enough to take outside. The neighborhood is also wide awake. Older boys play basketball at a hoop near the corner; other kids are riding bikes and yelling back and forth. Across the street, my neighbor Lori is on her front porch, rocking her youngest on her lap while talking on the telephone. Her older girls are on the front lawn turning cartwheels.

I go down the steps, pulling Jo's jacket over her little arms at the same time.

Lori sees me and comes down her steps too, still talking and rocking.

Lori could best be described as the neighborhood welcoming committee. She was the first one to greet us when we bought the house and, as a stay-at-home mom, is a consistent presence on the street. With short brown hair and a round, pretty face, she's also easy to talk to.

When Lori reaches the last step, she says her goodbyes to whomever she was talking to, turns off her phone, and puts her little boy on the ground. He toddles a few feet down the sidewalk and stops.

"Stay close," she says to her son while tickling Jo's chin.

"How are you guys doing?" she says.

Jo is sleepy faced and flushed from her nap, and her baby hair is wispy around her chubby face.

"We're good," I say. "How are you?"

Lori says she's good too, but she's got her eye on the street, like a traffic cop.

"Car!" she yells, so loud that it makes me step back from surprise.

The kids on the street move out of the way of the car, and those who were near the street are all temporarily paralyzed from her announcement. Once the car goes by, play resumes.

"Spencer went down to Malcolm's house," I say. "Steve's met them but I haven't. Are they cool?"

"Very cool," Lori says. "They're musicians."

I don't really get the connection between attentive parenting and being musical.

"Maybe I should check on him anyway," I say.

"You worry too much," Lori says. "He's fine and besides, everyone on this street looks out for each other's kids. It's one of our rules, remember?"

Lori is both talking to me and watching the street. She's dressed like she's ready to go to the gym, in a pair of sweatpants and a sweat top with a hood.

"Right, you said it takes a village," I say.

She tugs her sweat top down around her hips and gives me a full eye-contact moment.

"That's right," she says, "and we're the villagers. So relax. He's fine."

I rock side to side, a habitual movement that comes to me when I'm holding a child, but I wonder if it's not to comfort myself more than the baby. I'm not really sure about this whole village thing.

Lori's phone rings and she gets it on the second ring.

Her little boy ventures farther down the sidewalk and toward the street. As a villager, should I corral him back to his mother? I decide to head him off at the curb, but Lori hands me her phone.

"Me?" I say. "Who is it?"

"Leslie Cole," Lori whispers.

Leslie Cole is a playdate mom who lives a block away. Since we moved to this street, we haven't had a chance to get the boys together, but we keep saying we will. I figure she might be calling about that, but again, that's just odd. Why doesn't she call me at my house?

"I couldn't get you at your house," Leslie says. "I tried."

Her voice is high and strange.

"What's going on?" I say.

"Spencer was over here a little while ago," she says. "He was with two other boys and he had a knife. The three of them threatened Charlie with it and then ran away."

"No, no, that can't be right. Spencer's here, playing," I say. "He'd never go over to your house alone."

"Car!" Lori yells.

A couple of kids run from the middle of the street to the sidewalk until the car passes.

"Jennifer," Leslie says, "I'm telling you, it was Spencer and he was with these other kids I don't know."

"I am completely confused," I say. "My Spencer? Your Charlie?"

"Yes," Leslie says. "With two other boys who had a knife!"

I am without the ability to comprehend what Leslie is saying to me and cannot even form a response. I feel like the village idiot with Lori's phone in my hand.

Six months ago, before we lived here, I was pregnant with Jo. We had bought our new house but weren't going to move in for a while. I remember visiting the street and agreeing with Steve that the place seemed like a dream. Kids were running up and down the sidewalks, laughing and having a great time. Neighbors were chatting it up with each other, and Lori was even there, waving hello and telling us how great it was to live on that street. Everything sparkled in that fresh, new way of things that you haven't come to know yet.

That night I had a nightmare about our new house. I dreamt Spencer was playing with one of the neighbor boys. The two of them were holding a gun and then Spencer got shot.

I woke up immediately and lay in bed, trying not to cry even though it was impossible. The dream had been so vivid that I couldn't get the image of my dead son out of my head. All I could see was this snapshot of him lying in a pool of his own blood, his eyes open and his life gone.

I had to get up and see him alive and breathing and whole.

I sat by his bed for the longest time, looking at the smooth skin of his perfect face, taking in the details of his seamless features, and tried to calm myself.

Spencer's bear had fallen on the floor, and I picked him up, holding him against my growing stomach.

Moving wasn't as much my idea as it was Steve's. He never liked our busy street and wanted to be in a "real" neighborhood where kids could play on the street. For years he had plans to move, but I really liked our house. I liked how we could stay safely tucked away in the backyard of our house, I liked how we didn't have a bunch of pesky and invasive neighbors, and I liked our privacy.

Marriage is a series of compromises, though, and a real neighborhood was Steve's dream. Steve's happiness was important to me, and his dream became my dream.

That night, though, I realized I was really scared about moving. That street had twenty-three kids scattered among ten households. How could I possibly know all of those people and trust that Spencer would be safe? Then again, how could I deprive Spencer of playing with other kids?

It was all too much, I guess, and my dream proved that worry was bubbling deep inside the caves of my subconscious.

Spencer moved in his bed, turning from his side to his back, and he was lit by the shadows of his nightlight. I loved him more than I could ever imagine loving another being, and I'd do anything to keep him safe; at the same time, I knew I was losing the ability to keep him safe, and I didn't know what to do about that.

I watched him for a while longer and put the bear back into bed with him. I kissed his face, smelling that wonderful, clean little-boy smell, and then made myself go back to bed.

Without any explanation, I give the phone back to Lori and run down the sidewalk to Malcolm's house. Poor Josephine bounces on my hip, up and down, but is laughing for the ride. I run up the steps and knock on the front door.

"Come on," I say to the door, "come on."

Malcolm peeks out of the sheers that cover the door and I wave. He pulls the door open with both hands.

"Hey," I say, "you know me, Spencer's mom."

Malcolm's bangs hang halfway down over his eyes, and he moves his hand up in his hair and blows upwards at the same time, like he's winded or just worn out.

"I know," he says.

"Spencer's here, right?" I say.

"We're making a comic book," he says.

"Great," I say.

I can barely keep standing; I am so relieved and have to put my hand on the doorjamb for support.

Malcolm waves me in.

"Your mom is here!" Malcolm yells.

I step over the threshold and look around. It's a very nice house, but there is no evidence of an adult.

"Where's your mom?" I say.

"Upstairs," he says, "working."

I look up at the ceiling and Malcolm looks up too.

Spencer stomps around the corner, and he's got a mad look on his face.

I want to hug him, kiss him, shake him, yell at him, and start crying all at the same time. I shift Jo on my hip and put my hand out for him to take.

"We've got to go," I say.

"I just got here," he says. "I want to play."

"You've been here for more than an hour," I say, "and you are coming home, now."

Any other time, there would have been a fit, but Spencer must sense trouble. He lifts a hand to Malcolm.

"See ya," he says.

"Yeah," Malcolm says, "see you around."

I say goodbye to Malcolm and thank him for having Spencer; I even tell him to have his mother call me, but I am more focused on getting Spencer home.

Outside again, the village is in full swing. More kids are out; a couple more neighbors are out too, talking together. Steve is home and he's talking to Lori now.

When he sees me, he waves and I wave back, but I also toss a chin-up thing that says, *We've got trouble.*

Steve gets the message loud and clear.

A couple minutes later, we are all in the house, with us on the inside and the village on the outside. I close the door.

"What happened?" Steve says.

"Let's sit," I say.

I guide Spencer to the sofa. Steve sits in a chair, and I sit on the floor with Jo.

Afternoon sun comes through the windows at the back of the house, and even though the front door is closed, I can still hear all the kids playing and Lori yelling, "Car!"

"Tell us what happened over at Charlie's house today," I say.

Spencer's face goes blank like he has no idea, and then his eyes get wide. He's not old enough to have clear diction, and his words come out mashed together like he has marbles in his mouth. He does a good job telling the story. Frank had a knife; they wanted to show it to someone; Spencer told them about his friend Charlie; and they went over to his house.

"Frank said it would be okay," Spencer said.

Jo is on her back, rolling one way and then the other, and I watch her because if I do anything else, my head will explode. I just can't believe what I am hearing Spencer say, which isn't much different from what Leslie said, but I will myself not to react at all, since, in some cases, an overreaction is as bad as the actual act. Instead, I look at Steve for what to do next.

Steve moves his hand over his jaw.

"How big was this knife?" he says.

Spencer holds his hands open to show what looks to be a butcher knife.

"Did it fold?" Steve says.

"It had a cover for the blade," Spencer says.

Steve nods like he gets it and then sets his sights on me.

"How did this happen?" he says.

"Excuse me?" I say.

"Weren't you watching him?" he says.

All of a sudden, we've shifted from being a team to something else, and there is a hot spark up my back, like I need to defend myself.

"I was," I say, "but he was outside for a while, and I asked him to stay in front of the house."

"Why wasn't he in here with you?" he says.

"He wanted to be outside, Steve," I say.

"Sometimes he can't be outside," Steve says. "Someone has to watch him."

I have all but forgotten the baby on the floor. She grabs for my hands, and I offer my fingers for her to hold, thankful for the distraction. Jo locks her hands around my fingers and pulls to sit up.

Spencer kicks his heel up and down against the sofa, his arms wide over the cushions. He looks like a coat that someone has tossed on the sofa and forgotten about.

"Look," I say, "you weren't here with him; he was crazy to be outside in this weather; I asked him to stay in front of the house; I checked him every ten minutes. What else could I do?"

Steve shakes his head like I really screwed up, like this is my fault; and in a way, I guess it is. If I had made Spencer come in, this wouldn't have happened at all; but then, I'm mad too.

"You can blame me for this, Steve," I say, "but this is what you wanted for him, a neighborhood where he would be safe to play with other kids. I trusted that he was safe, and I trusted that he would listen to me, but I guess that didn't happen. I guess it's good we know that this is a place where kids have knives and who knows what else. Maybe they have guns or light fires. I don't know."

"There wasn't a fire," Spencer says.

Spencer is so serious, I can't help laughing at him, which is nice, since it eases away the tension for a minute.

"And we were just kidding," Spencer says. "It wasn't for real, it was like a joke."

Steve does this thing where he rubs his whole face with his hands, up and down, up and down.

"I can't believe this would happen here," he says. "It's one of the best neighborhoods in Portland, for God's sake."

Josephine is on her back again and reaching for a stuffed lion. I hand it to her.

"Now we know," I say.

I am stinging from the assault of blame and the residual guilt that comes with being at fault, and Steve stews in how this isn't the ideal neighborhood after all, but I realize that we have to move now.

I put together a plan of action in which Spencer and I will go to Leslie's house so he can apologize, and Steve will watch the baby and call Frank's parents and get to the bottom of the knife issue.

Twenty minutes later, Spencer and I walk back to our house, and behind us is Leslie's house and Spencer's apology.

"I'm sorry we scared Charlie," Spencer says. "We were just kidding."

"Thank you, Spencer," Leslie says, and she is smiling, but who knows what is behind that smile. I'm sure she thinks I am raising some kind of murderer, and who knows, maybe I am.

As we walk together, under the branches of oaks and elms, I can't help thinking of that dream I had all those months ago. I can't help wondering what it all meant, and if maybe it's not time for me to face up to my disgust about guns and violence and the deep fears that I have about them. Guns and knives are everywhere, and my kid is one of those people who wants to get ahold of them. Maybe he needs to feel powerful; maybe he wants to taste danger; maybe he's having some past life memory of being a warrior, who knows. It's part of who he is, though, and I guess I need to find a way to face it.

I wonder if this is how it started with those boys who took guns to school and shot their classmates. Were those boys like my sweet Spencer or the jaded neighbor boy, Frank? Did they have knives when they were seven and make death threats? In ten years, will Spencer graduate to making bombs from directions he finds on the Internet or stockpiling guns in the basement? One day, will I be the mother on the news who looks at the camera and says, "I don't know what happened; he was such a sweet little boy"?

The air smells heavy, like it's going to rain. While we walk, I touch his head and rest my hand on his shoulder. He's still so small.

"Once when I was five," I say, "my dad pulled my pants down and spanked me with his belt."

Spencer looks up and his eyes are wide and round.

"Am I getting a spanking?" he says.

"Do you think I should spank you?" I say.

We stop walking and Spencer shakes his head, absolutely not.

"We don't spank," he says.

"Why don't we spank?" I say.

"Because hitting is wrong," he says.

"That's right," I say.

Wind blows the leaves in the trees, and the sound is like a polite audience clapping for a performance.

I kneel down to look at him and squeeze his shoulders.

"A lot of things are wrong," I say. "Leaving our block is wrong. Talking about killing is wrong, even if it is a game. Playing with knives is very wrong, and the next time you see a knife, you must tell me or a grownup."

I keep my eyes steady on his eyes the way I do when it's serious.

"Do you understand me?" I say.

Spencer nods like yes, he understands.

I stand up and we start walking again, crossing the intersection to our block.

"What should we do for a punishment?" I say.

Spencer looks up at the sky, taking it all very seriously, and finally he speaks with authority and confidence.

"No dessert," he says, "and no TV."

"For tonight?" I say. "Or for a few days?"

"For tonight and tomorrow night," he says.

"Fair enough," I say.

We take it slow, walking by a long row of chestnut trees with trunks so big, I could put my arms around them and still my hands wouldn't touch.

There are so many things I want to say to him right now. I want to tell him about my dream. I want to tell him about the boys who shot their classmates and paid the price of losing their freedom. I want to tell him how dangerous the world is in general. I want to tell him how scary this day was, how he could have been hurt or worse, killed. I want to tell him how he could have hurt someone else too. I want to tell him to be careful, to be safe, to be smart for those times when I can't be there.

At the corner, we turn on our block again, and Spencer pulls his hand free.

"Can I run the rest of the way home?" he says.

"Okay," I say.

He takes off with arms and legs pumping, his chin out like an arrow, pointing him in the direction he wants to go.

That warm, sweaty feeling of our touch is on my skin, and I close my fingers into my palm.

Our so-called village is quiet now, all the kids and grownups in their houses for the night; the white flower petals that were all over the street have been shoved into gutters by the force of wind and passing cars.

At our house, Spencer disappears up the steps, and I hear him yell, "Dad, I'm home."

I walk the rest of the way alone, my hand closed tight as if I can hold the feeling of Spencer there forever.

Becoming a Boy

ROBIN
BRADFORD

I am taking my son and two friends he's known since preschool out on New Year's Eve day. Our first stop is the children's museum, where there will be a noon balloon drop for those who can't stay up till midnight. As the boys alternately amble and race through the bat exhibit, I realize with a small sadness they've become nearly too old for most of the displays. They sense it too. Their energy dissipates and they look slightly confused. But soon they encounter something they can relate to: the tornado exhibit, where you push a button and create your own vortex. I talk about the hot air on the top and cool air on the bottom (or is it the other way around?), but what captures their imagination is this whirling cloud's power of destruction. They suggest things that could be thrown into the whorl: a toy army man, a plastic fork, a flaming match, a poison dart.

Being around growing boys is like observing a miniature tornado. Their bodies and minds are forces of energy taking in information, spinning it into something new, and spitting it back out before roaring on. I

117

wonder if it is the same with girls. I remember only rare glimpses of my power as a girl of eight—riding my bike in the wind, pricking fingers with my best friend, writing a poem the teacher put up on the board.

Granted, I was a genuine girlie-girl. I rode my tricycle wearing a plaid dress with a neck frill. Summer found me sporting sleeveless A-lines with matching bloomers. My all-time favorite attire was a sundress spotted with tiny rosebuds, with a keyhole back that my mother sewed up during our poor patch. My mother believed that since she was divorced, a rarity in 1960s Oklahoma, people would judge us. So she made sure I was always the picture of a young lady.

The air boys breathe seems laced with something different from anything I ever knew. They inhale entitlement and energy and exhale exuberance and explosiveness. As the countdown for the balloon drop finally begins at the museum, the balloons fall, red and fat. In the end it is the babies who make the most noise, the girls who gather the colorful confetti, and the boys who get all the balloons—and pop them.

When I turned thirty, I went to a psychic to have my wide-open single-girl fortune told. Sitting across from me at her dining room table, Mrs. Garcia laid out some cards in a row and turned them over slowly, announcing that I would travel west, attend a wedding, and work in the movies. Then she took my hand in hers, examining my palm as if it were a strange object. Stroking a hair-thin crease on the side of my hand, below my pinkie finger, she said, "Your first child will be your husband's spiritual sister."

Though none of her other predictions came true in any obvious way, four years later when I became pregnant, I knew that the cells dividing inside me, quickly devoting themselves to this or that purpose, would

soon form a brain, a stomach, a vagina. I didn't doubt that what was forming inside was a tiny replica of myself.

My wish for a girl was understandable—I knew everything about
Girl World and precious little about boys. Being raised alone by my single
mother (with a female cat), I was a prodigy at girldom. What to wear to
make him remember you. What to do if he doesn't call. How to go from
office to cocktails with just a switch of a scarf. What sort of swimsuit for a
pear shape. How to reduce undereye swelling, whiten teeth, and soften feet
using products commonly found in the kitchen. Though I would later consider this 1970s simplicity bunk, the knowledge has never left me, like the
words to old John Denver songs and a craving for marshmallow creme.

Boys, however, were a bona fide mystery. I had studied the side-
view line drawing of the penis, urethra, and testicles in the book provided by my mother, but I didn't stop being aghast at a penis and its
ever-changing parts until I was at least twenty-three. Before I started
dating, the guys in my life came from history books and literature—
presidents and protagonists—not counting scattered visits from my
father, who took me to the zoo and out for fried-shrimp dinners. Then
I toiled for a dozen years in the dating mine, amassing knowledge about
the male species from the men I slept with, a handful of gay friends, and
a few other men I had invisible crushes on. The facts were inconclusive:
Men didn't shower enough or reeked of too-sweet cologne; they made
things with their hands or destroyed them with their drinking; they loved
me until I screamed or just made me scream. Eventually, I found my own
perfect specimen of guydom in a man who has long hair, wears purple,
hates football, cries at movies, and whips up an addictive chocolate pud-
di..g. Once I married him, I didn't need to know anything more about the
Y chromosome. Or so I thought.

After a quick turn in the "earthquake house," a small room at the museum with a floor that rocks to a rumble of static, I take the boys to an old-fashioned burger place with grubby picnic tables out back. They sit elbow to elbow, unwrapping their burgers while I deal out napkins. The couples and families at nearby tables look over at them with admiration. *Look! Boys eating!* We are as patriotic as football and SUVs. A line of boys devouring burgers inspires pride. If you feed them, they will grow. And when they grow, they will be president; they will run the companies, know the answers, fix what's broken, and invest wisely.

True, strangers might also smile if I had a row of ponytailed girls facing me with their appetites. But they would be admiring the girls for their good manners and their ability to emulate women. The girls might smile back or toss their hair. Boys don't need strangers' admiration. They just keep on doing whatever they're doing. Sadly, we don't admire girls for their sheer appetites. Sure, they might run companies and they'll certainly know important things, and they might even be *vice* president, but a girl is admired for the woman she will become. And that means the impression she will create when she walks into a room. As a girl, I grew up learning to hide the fierceness of my appetites. As the mother of a boy, I've learned to assert my desires, chase what I want, and hit a backyard home run.

Of course, all boys are not the same. Even in this bunch, there are differences. Griffin is tall, blond, and smart enough to spell *esophagus*, then tell you how one works. Given to impulse, he is suspicious, clever, and loves pickles. Webster is a little shorter but much smaller. At the museum his favorite activity is constructing a car out of toilet paper rolls and yogurt cups. His favorite part of lunch is the french fries, which he slides through the ketchup with his slim fingers. My son, Cope, can't eat cheese. He believes lactose intolerance and dyslexia have ruined his life. He is dramatic, creative, and passionate. He recently performed a play at home about ninja warriors, in which he played all the parts. Yet these boys have at least one thing in common. When I mention we're not far from the city park that has a giant playscape by the creek, they gather our far-flung trash and toss it into the receptacle faster than the most efficient of sanitation workers.

The world of boys is a rough, exotic country. I entered it quickly, agreeing to have my son circumcised when he was less than a day old. I sent him down the bright hall with my husband to do their mysterious men's work, the sort of toil women truly can't understand, while I visited politely with my midwife and listened desperately with my nipples for his cries. There were none. I aspire to be as brave as he one day.

At first there was no real difference. I compared with other postpartum moms in my yoga class: Our newborns had the same dried raisin umbilical stump; the same strong mouth, fisted feet, marigold poo, blind squall. My son was neither boy nor girl, just new. But one morning we woke too early, two months having passed, and when I opened my eyes to his bright face and wiggling body next to mine, he was changed. He had outgrown all his sexless newborn clothes. His new miniature weightlifter's body demanded stretchy suits bearing fire trucks or dogs. Suddenly it was spring, and the tree in the backyard became an umbrella of leaves. We swayed in the hammock below, singing "Ten Little Indians," the only boyish song I knew. It was not long before he displayed a talent that only men have—the ability to pee in one's own face.

Soon I was lying on the floor, a highway for his traffic. He rolled his Hot Wheels down my shoulder, arm, hip, thigh, calf, foot, all the while making a *putt-putt* noise with his wet lips. A line of tiny wheels massaged my tired body. For the first time, I felt adored for who I am. I had done nothing to earn his adoration—no high heels, push-up bras, glitter, or giggling. This young man loved the messy me, the one who hadn't had a shower, who sang off-key, and who wore glasses because she was too tired to put in her contacts. (His father had long professed this same love, but it was the unbearded one who taught me to *accept* this gift.)

When I grew up, girls stayed inside when the weather was foul. They spun in circles wearing white skates with pink pompons. My world was separate from Legos, Matchbox cars, army men, and dozens of other "boy toys." Now when my son puts on his skates, I choose to leave my novel unread on the bench and join him. I'm the one saying that if we hike in the rain, we'll have the trail to ourselves. And I even have a couple Matchbox cars of my own. There's no way I'll ever know what it's *really* like to be a boy—or a man!—but mothering my son has grown parts of my brain and personality that were previously untended.

At the park, the bright afternoon passes under the leafless trees. I read just a few pages of my trusty book. I can't help watching these boys move through the world. As they race across the expanse of the playground, huddle in the secret space beneath a play fire truck, and step from rock to rock across the cold water, I watch them with the intensity of a girl in love. I remember this feeling, sitting on the edge of the basketball court in junior high, watching the boys fling their bodies into the air and dance the ball among their feet. Back then, I just wanted one of them to notice me, talk to me, ask me to the Spring Ball. But crouching on a hard rock by the edge of the creek, I think now that perhaps my longing was confused. Maybe I wanted to *be* one of those flying boys who slung sweat off his back like a horse. For me, it took having a boy to become one.

I push off my shoes and stuff in my socks. The water is so cold on my ankles it hurts. As green-headed ducks drift by and the sun glints blades onto the water and three boys with their pants rolled to their knees balance on mossy stones, I step in deeper and cringe. A boy can do that to you.

Reading to My Son

KATE
STAPLES

I've always viewed the world through a spine-shaped prism. My single punishable act of high school rebellion was a refusal to let the principal pry the banned book *Are You There God? It's Me, Margaret* from my sweaty palms. I broke up with a college boyfriend who called Jane Austen overrated, and I later learned to gauge the potential of boyfriend material based on the guy's top five desert island books. I comfort myself with the notion that at least books are a healthy obsession—though they are an obsession nonetheless and, like many manias, must be managed carefully lest they commandeer your life and leave you with all the interpersonal skills of Captain Ahab at a Sea World.

Like many of my obsessions, this one came courtesy of my upbringing. I grew up in a family of kids who would, by and large, rather read than talk to one another. My sister went for trashy epics; one brother lived in biographies; my other brother still brags about his summer with Proust; I leaned toward contemporary fiction. On summer days we'd align our lawn chairs with the sun and gorge on print, stopping only to adjust the angle of our chairs. To this day, I recall less about my siblings' friends or whom they dated than I do about their favorite books. A few years ago, when we sold our childhood house, most of the bickering was over who got the leather-bound Dickens collection and who went home with the bound *New Yorkers* from the sixties through the nineties.

As kids, even given our voracity for books, we could not begin to touch our parents' proficiency. Given ample ammunition and a time machine, my father, a history buff, could have won any major historical conflict single-handedly with his encyclopedic knowledge of battles and strategies—though he was largely outmatched in the bed wars, an ugly and ongoing offensive waged by my mother's political biographies and *Life* magazines, gathering forces to invade his side of the bed.

It's not surprising that her bedside reading material piled up, given my mother's active schedule. She worked outside the home, which was unusual for that time, and, at least it seemed to me as a kid, she was rarely around. The one activity she did insist on was the nightly reading of the bedtime story. Though I'm unclear on whether it's a true memory or merely inspired by the pictures my father took of my mother reading to me, I recall her hovering over my crib with a book during a time in my life when my finest expression of literary appreciation was an enthusiastic spit-up. Later I remember her indulgence, repeating *Madeleine* and *The Cat in the Hat* as many times as I insisted, or reading large chunks of *The Chronicles of Narnia* and Nancy Drew mysteries until I fell asleep. Since she was often on her way out somewhere, she was usually wearing a party dress, which I frequently mistook for pajamas.

It was our only reliable time together. When I think about being on the receiving end of mothering, it often involves illustrations and the crinkle of turning pages. I remember her perfume, the half-moon of white at the end of her unpolished fingernails, the feel of her hairsprayed curls against my cheek. I will never forget the way she said "green eggs and ham," as if they were a four-star delicacy. She breathed life into the settings and the characters, until they seemed to inhabit my bedroom and infiltrate my imagination. My best friends were, at various times, Madeleine, Harriet the Spy, Pippi Longstocking, and each of the girls from Little Women. For many years I actually believed I *was* Nancy Drew, and I attempted to solve many neighborhood mysteries, including what Mr. Johnson was doing sneaking into the garden shed with those magazines and why Mrs. Perkins wore sunglasses on cloudy days. My investigative career came to an abrupt end the day I followed a suspicious sound to my sister's room, where she and her boyfriend were conducting their own investigation and had forgotten to lock the door.

My sister's wrath aside, reading allowed me to explore various identities without risk. I could be a wild orphan, a nineteenth-century settler, a little French girl with a very bad attitude. Disappointingly, few dead bodies were found in our neighborhood during my Nancy Drew phase, though that didn't deter me from skulking around as if the killer might still be at large, thinking I knew too much.

The day I found out I was pregnant, I thought of the books first. I began canvassing the children's bookstores, getting a feel for who had the classics and where I could find the best selection of innovative titles. In no time, I was lost in the stories of my childhood. It was like a class reunion to which only the kids you liked were invited. The prospect of holding that tiny body in my arms was nearly eclipsed by that of sharing these worlds with my child: *The Secret Garden, Harriet the Spy.* I imagined my body wedged into a tiny bed, one arm wrapped around those little shoulders, the other holding open the book as I read "Please Mommy, just one more chapter!" of the latest Nancy Drew. Nancy was like a sister to me, her only irritating quality being an inexplicable attachment to the smarmy Ned. I looked forward to finding out what I'd missed in the last thirty years or so since I'd helped her solve a mystery. That first day, I started stocking up on the essentials and made mental notes of future purchases, when the words became as important as the pictures.

The news that I was carrying a boy was hardly a disappointment. Frilly dresses and patent leather shoes were as far from my mind as bikinis and dieting. In fact, I'd been such a tomboy growing up that my mother still bristles at the memory of my performance of Mary in the school Christmas pageant, with the flash of blue jeans under my dress. My bedroom was filled with sports posters; it was a dream of mine to play wide receiver for the Minnesota Vikings. Behind reading, my most-anticipated active parenting activities included touch football and shooting hoops one on one. So it wasn't as if I feared I couldn't relate to a boy, but still . . . the Hardy Boys?

I was being silly, my mother told me. You'll read him whatever you'd read a girl. Nancy Drew, she claimed, was a big hit with both my brothers, an assertion that relieved me until a quick check with my brothers drew derisive guffaws. One swore he'd been obsessed with the American Revolution by the time he was six months old. The other boasted an enduring fascination with the explorations of Lewis and Clarke. And though I suspect the truth lies somewhere in between my mother's memories of open-minded sons and the sons' confidence in their early intellectual prowess, it was clear that my rosy nostalgic images of my son running around the neighborhood mimicking Harriet the Spy might be subject to a reality check.

Then I tried to convince myself that there are no such things as girl books and boy books. Everyone loves Harry Potter, right? I was above such artificial forced gender identification, a construct pressed on us by society's need to categorize people. Then again, I wasn't out there scouting the shelves of dolls, and I was pretty sure I wouldn't be dressing him in pink sweaters. Out of curiosity, I began looking at the sorts of books that were associated with boy interests: trucks, trains, rockets, sports. They involved either moving parts or groups of kids rallying around a ball.

Knowing how books helped to shape my identity, I began to wonder if my son's path would necessarily include tractors and robots sent to annihilate Earth, themselves annihilated by a balloon-chested superhero in red tights. I knew I was being ridiculous. Boys weren't all like the mini Cro-Magnons I'd grown up with, stuffing firecrackers into the mouths of frogs and appreciating *The Cat in the Hat* primarily for its offensive aerial properties during a temper tantrum. Boys were as individual as books, and my boy would write his own story. However, it's one thing to know that you're being ridiculous and quite another to put a stop to it.

Owen took to books early. His favorite, a Richard Russo novel of academia, had a shiny red cover that felt good against his gums. His content appreciation commenced a few months later, when he latched on to *Goodnight Moon*. He would point out the moon, giggle at the kittens, clap his hands at the red balloon. When I was done, he would cry until I read it again. And again. Things were looking good.

Around the year mark, he stopped taking an interest in *Goodnight Moon*. More accurately, he started taking an active disinterest in it by hurling it across the room. Sensing a watershed moment, I began to read from

Madeleine. No dice. He pushed at the cover and, when I wouldn't give up, kicked it and cried. I spread out all his books on the floor so he could make his own informed choice.

He picked out the usual suspects—a dog who eats his way through the alphabet, a duck running for president—then dug through the pile for a picture book of trucks. I pushed it aside and took out *Green Eggs and Ham*. He followed along with interest to the end. Then he reached for the trucks. I countered with *Where the Wild Things Are*. He loved it. Then he wanted the trucks. The more I kept trying to distract him from the trucks, the more he wanted them. *Here we go*, I thought, opening to a large red dump truck.

Owen clambered on my lap and pressed his face up to the wheels. He rubbed them and squealed with delight. The shiny yellow dump bed got an even bigger reaction, and he was in near ecstasy over the silver tailpipe. Flipping through the pages by himself, pausing, and going back, he occasionally looked up at me as if to say, "Check this out!"

And there it was. Everything that I'd wanted for him was in that look: the wonder, the joy, and the passion for something just beyond his burgeoning imagination so that he had to stretch out to take it in. It didn't matter that it was a truck. It could have been a barn, a spaceship, a dollhouse. What did matter was the way he had momentarily let go of reality and thrown himself into another world. He was inside that truck, driving it, honking its horn, or maybe just sitting in the cab, taking in the view.

Now Owen's reading preferences change on a dime. But at this young age, books have already made their mark. The sight of a Dr. Seuss book is frequently the only cure for a tantrum; days begin and end with his little fingers rummaging through the bookcase, checking the familiar spines. No matter how many times he's read a book, it still has the power to capture his imagination as he crawls inside its pages. He might not even realize he's being transported, but I can see it in his eyes. And I'm starting to learn that the important thing is not where he goes, but his desire to make the trip. And, for as long as he lets me, I'm happy to go with him.

Samuel

SUSAN
ITO

I remember almost nothing about that first pregnancy except the way that it ended. I remember a walk along the grassy trails of Sea Ranch, the wild wind, my bursting energy. I was wearing my husband John's blue jeans because mine didn't fit anymore.

In August, a trip to the beach with his brother's family. I swelled in the humidity like a sponge, my breasts enormous, my face squishy with fluid. "Look at me," I said, frowning in the mirror. "You look wonderful," he said. It wasn't what I was talking about.

John, a doctor, went from that family vacation to El Salvador, heading a medical delegation to the war zone of Guazapa, under the volcano. My father-in-law disapproved, told me outright that John was abandoning me. But I was proud. While he was in Central America, I drove to Davis to help load a containerful of wheelchairs, crutches, and medicine bound for Nicaragua. On the way home, I couldn't lace my sneakers. My feet were the size of small footballs.

I picked him up at the airport, saying, "Don't you think I look fat?"

"You're pregnant, sweetheart," he said. "That's how you're supposed to look."

Sunday morning. September 17, 1989. I had gained thirteen pounds in a week. I pulled out the pregnancy book. In red print, it said, *Call the doctor if you gain more than three pounds in one week. If your face or hands or feet are swollen. If. If. If.* I checked them off. While John was in the shower, I called my obstetrician and friend, Lisa. I whispered under the sound of running water, "I think something is wrong."

Lisa's voice was so smooth, so calm. "Swelling is very common," she said, "but it would be a good idea to get a blood pressure check. Can John do it?"

We stopped by his office, two blocks from the restaurant we had decided on for dinner. We were planning a movie, a bookstore, our usual date. I hopped onto the exam table, held out my arm. I couldn't wait to get to la Méditerranée. My mouth had been dreaming spanakopita all day.

I heard the Velcro tearing open on the cuff, felt its smooth blue band wrapping around me. I swung my feet and smiled up at John, the stethoscope around his neck, loved this small gesture of his taking care of me. I felt the cuff tightening, the pounding of my heart echoing up and down my fingers, through my elbow.

The expression on his face I will never forget, the change in color from pink to ash, as if he had died standing at my side. "Lie down," he said quietly. "Lie down on your left side. *Now.*"

The numbers were all wrong, two hundred plus, over and over again, his eyes darkening as he watched the mercury climb on the wall. He shook his head. "What's Lisa's phone number?"

His voice was grim on the phone—numbers, questions, ideas. He told me to go into the tiny bathroom and pee into a cup. "We've got to dipstick your urine, see if there's any protein."

I sat on the toilet and listened to him crash through the cupboards, knocking over samples of ulcer pills, brochures about stomach cancer, looking for a container of thin paper tabs. I gave him the paper cup, the gold liquid cloudy and dense. The dipstick changed color the way his face did, from white to powdery blue to sky to deep indigo. "No," he whispered. "No, no, goddammit, no."

I asked what, over and over, not believing, as he pulled me out the door, across the street to the hospital. He pounded the buttons of the elevator, pulled me flying to the nurses' station, spat numbers at them. I thought, *Don't be a bully, nurses hate doctors who are bullies*; but they scattered like quail, one of them on the phone, another pushing me, stumbling, into a room. There were three of them, pulling at my clothes, my shoes; the blood pressure cuff again; the shades were drawn; they moved so swiftly, with such seriousness.

I had a new doctor now. Lisa, obstetrician of the normal, was off my case, and I was assigned a neonatologist named Weiss. He was perfectly bald, with thick glasses, and wooden clogs, a soft voice.

A squirt of blue gel on my belly for the fetal monitor, the galloping sound of hoofbeats, the baby riding a wild pony inside me. What a relief to hear that sound, although I didn't need the monitor, I could feel the baby punching at my liver.

There was a name for what I had. Preeclampsia. Ahh. Well, preeclampsia was certainly better than eclampsia, and as long as it was pre, then they could stop it. And what was eclampsia? An explosion of blood pressure, a flood of protein poisoning the blood, kidney failure, the vessels in spasm, a stroke, seizures, blindness, death. But I didn't have any of those things. I had preeclampsia. It felt safe.

They slipped a needle into my wrist, hung a bag of magnesium sulfate. This is to prevent seizures, they said. You may feel a little hot. As the first drops of the drug slipped into my bloodstream, I felt a flash of electricity inside my mouth. My tongue was baking. My scalp prickled, burning, and I threw up onto the sheets. I felt as if I was being microwaved.

I was wheeled down to radiology. Pictures of the baby onscreen, waving, treading water. A real child, not a pony or a fish. The x-ray tech, a woman with curly brown hair and a red Coca-Cola t-shirt, asked, "Do you want to know the sex?" I sat up. "There you go." She pointed. A flash between the legs, like a finger. A boy. I nearly leapt off the gurney. "John! Did you see? A boy! It's Samuel!" Sahm-*well*, the Spanish pronunciation, named after our surrogate father in Nicaragua, the most dignified man we knew.

He didn't want to look, couldn't celebrate having a son. He knew so much more than I did.

Weiss came to stand next to my bed. Recited numbers slowly. Baby needs two more weeks for viability. He's already too small, way too small. "But you . . ." He looked at me sadly, shook his head. "You can't survive two weeks without stroke, seizures, worse." He meant I could die.

"What are the chances . . . ?" Doctors are always talking percentages.

"Less than 10 percent, less than 5 percent." The space between his fingers shrunk into nothing.

This is how they said it. I was toxemic, poisoned by pregnancy.

My only cure was to not be pregnant anymore. The baby needed two more weeks, just fourteen days.

I looked at John hopefully. "I can wait. It will be all right."

"Honey. Your blood pressure is through the roof. Your kidneys are shutting down. You are *on the verge of having a stroke.*"

I actually smiled at him. I actually said that having a stroke at twenty-nine would not be a big deal. I was a physical therapist; I knew about rehab. I could rehabilitate myself. I could walk with a cane. Lots of people do it. I had a bizarre image of leaning on the baby's carriage, supporting myself the way elderly people use a walker.

We battled back and forth through the night. "I'm not going to lose this baby," I said.

"I'm not going to lose *you.*"

He won.

I lay with my hands on my belly all night, feeling Samuelito's limbs turning this way and that. There was nothing inside me that could even think of saying goodbye.

September 18, 1989. Another day of magnesium sulfate, the cuff that inflated every five minutes, the fetal monitor booming through the room. No change in status for either of us.

I signed papers of consent, my hand moving numbly across the paper, my mind screaming, I do *not* consent, I do *not*, I do not.

In the evening, Weiss's associate entered with a tray, a syringe, a nurse with mournful eyes.

"It's just going to be a bee sting," he said.

And it was, a small tingle, quick pricking bubbles, under my navel;

and then a thing like a tiny drinking straw that went in and out with a barely audible pop. It was so fast. I thought, *I love you, I love you, you must be hearing this, please hear me.* And then a Band-Aid was unwrapped, with its plastic smell of childhood, and spread onto my belly.

"All done," he said. All done.

My child was inside swallowing the fizzy drink, and it bubbled against his tiny tongue like a bud, the deadly soda pop.

This is what it was. A drug, injected into my womb, a drug to stop his heart. To lay him down to sleep, so he wouldn't feel what would happen the next day, the terrible terrible thing that would happen. "Evacuation" is what it is called in medical journals.

Evacuees are what the Japanese Americans were called when they were ripped from their homes, tagged like animals, flung into the desert. Evacuated, exiled, thrown away.

I lay on my side pinching the pillowcase. I wondered if he would be startled by the drug's taste, if it was bitter, or strange, or just different from the salt water he was used to. I prayed that it wouldn't be noxious, not like the magnesium sulfate, that it wouldn't hurt. That it would be fast.

John sat next to the bed and held one hand as I pressed the other against my belly. I looked over his shoulder into the dark slice of night between the heavy curtains. Samuel, Samuelito, jumped against my hand once. He leaped through the space into the darkness and then was gone.

All gone.

I have two other children now, both daughters. I love them with every cell in my body. And yet I do not forget that son, small cowboy, the way he galloped through me. There is still a part of me that believes that I failed the test of motherhood, the law that says your child comes before you, even if it means death. I look at my girls, the life that fills this family, and I think, none of this would be here. But still.

I wonder about our life with a boy, what it would have been. Now John often steps into the tension-filled space between my teenage daughter and me, as we work out our complicated mother-daughter dance. I wonder if he and Sam, Samuel, Samuelito, would have had this flinty hardness between them. I wonder if they would have played sports together, if they would have gone camping and fishing.

I have looked at a thousand boys, from toddlers to young men, since that day in 1989, and none of them have come close to the perfection of that unlived life, that beautiful son who never took a breath. I know how completely unfair it is, and yet I do it, have done it over and over: Our Sam, our Sammy, would never have pointed a stick like a weapon, would never have pulled the legs from an insect. He would have been cheerful, affectionate, bouncy and athletic, but not aggressive. He would have been an avid reader. He would have loved to learn, but not in a nerdy way. He would have been easy with his friends, sweet with his mother, bonded with his father. He would have grown up to be a camp counselor, a scientist, a pediatrician.

How much simpler it is to love a ghost, an angel of a child than one who is troublesomely human and alive.

The night his heart ceased to beat, I had an image of him that I flash to even now. I could see the person he would one day grow into, tousled, with dark, damp almost-curls stuck to his forehead. But he wouldn't smell bad, no: He would smell alive, human. A slightly torn, stretched-out t-shirt, something faded with a clever, ironic saying on it. He would have just stopped shooting hoops in the brick courtyard, resting at the bottom of the rickety, age-worn stairs. He would be drinking Coke from an old-fashioned green glass bottle like someone from a well-directed commercial. He would stop to look at me, in an instant of unembarrassed sweetness.

None of this is true.

If Samuel had lived, he would have smelled bad. He would have sworn and slammed the door and left his foul socks underneath the couch. He would have had times of sullenness. He would have fought with members of his family. He would have been far from perfect, as we all are. He would have been a complex, living person with qualities that are, at this moment, absolutely unknowable.

There are a million questions that will forever go unanswered. I wonder how I would fare as the mother of a boy. I am innately unathletic, and squeamish around the amphibians and insects that so many boys seem to love. But is that just a stereotype? Thinking that he would have grown up to be an athletic, snake-loving type of boy?

I often wonder how things would be different if he had survived that blast of preeclampsia and been born that September in 1989. He would have been miniscule, no larger than a baked potato. There would have been months in a neonatal intensive-care unit; possible (no, probable) complications. He might very well have had disabilities, from mild to unthinkably severe. And what kind of mother would this have made me? Heartbroken? Overwhelmed? Hoveringly protective?

When my daughters were born healthy, I was intensely grateful just that they were alive. It gave me the sense that they had made it through their uterine gauntlet and could thus dodge anything. Instead of becoming the hovering, worrying mother I might have been with a little preemie like Samuel, I became oddly relaxed. I didn't fret and cling like some other parents I knew. I let them go off to sleepaway circus camp when they were seven years old and most of their classmates hadn't even mastered one-night sleepovers. Perhaps, knowing that one of my children had already been taken from me, I believed that the powers that be wouldn't dream of taking another.

I've heard so often that parenting boys is utterly different from parenting girls, and I can only imagine the ways in which this might be true in our family. I know that sometimes the concentration of estrogen in the air can be stifling, and that the drama meter around here feels like it is permanently set to high. Would this have been different with a boy, and particularly with a boy named Samuel?

I wonder what kind of brother he would have been. I know that his sisters could not possibly be more different—physically or temperamentally. Would he have been dark and intense like our elder girl, or fair and mellow like the younger?

The questions swirl around and around; they break apart like atoms and produce even more questions. The answers are infinite and untouchable.

In the end, all I can really know about this child is that he would have been a boy. And he would have been loved.

THE VELVET
UNDERGROUND

Entering the Den of Math

GWENDOLEN
GROSS

Jacob, our five-year-old, is awake absurdly early, rummaging in his room for entertainment. From our room we hear shuttle, scuff, the crash of the Magna Doodle, a recitation of equations and answers, and a decisive "I'm so good at math!" He's administering and acing his own exam. Soon he'll want company other than his Kooshie toys, which have no doubt been instructed to sit and listen, or be sent to time-out, several times each by now. It's 6 AM, and it's the weekend. It's my turn to get the kids up, so I enter the Den of Math in my robe and sunglasses, because Jacob likes the overhead light on as soon as possible, and I don't. Sometimes he even covers his own eyes, states, "That hurts my eyes," but he wants illumination.

I am from a medical family. I grew up with *New England Journal of Medicine* as bathroom reading, and while I have developed a healthy twenty-first-century skepticism and open-mindedness to things spiritual, I do generally believe in science. So the first time I was pregnant, my husband and I decided it would be just fine to find out "what it was" when I had an ultrasound. But Jacob didn't turn to the low-quality camera, so the answer to our question was "We actually can't tell." That was fine. We bought yellow footie pajamas, white bunny onesies. The posters we had dry mounted showed Noah's Ark and baby penguins. I didn't care for pink anyway, I was sure (this would change with the second child). My mother was certain I was having a girl, but then, she had three. The assertive declarations of casual observers and those maddening pregnancy gropers who pat your belly without permission were split between gender predictions. I didn't care.

Then Jacob was born and I noticed I did care—I loved having a little boy, tiny man, infant equipped with all the parts and genetic instructions for maleness. And once I was over the initial stun of sleeplessness (and into the continuing drudge of sleeplessness, tempered with exquisite love), I started imagining him older, as one does with babies. I imagined him as the kind of boy who knows girls are equals; the teen with female friends as well as male; then a kind man, a good man, the kind of man who knows better than to be a heartbreaker, despite his looks. As a newborn, Jacob looked quite a bit like my dad, with my husband's grin, and he cherished being read to, being outside—maybe he would be a naturalist, a scientist, a writer, perhaps. I got ahead of myself.

When Jacob was two and a half, I was pregnant again. As when I was pregnant with Jacob, I threw up with stunning frequency. I threw up because I thought about food. I threw up because it was the middle of the night. One morning, we went downstairs and I threw up because there was something unpleasant just outside the trash can and I decided to pick it up: an egg bagel, rather old, with some penicillin-blue mold carpeting its hole. *I should have let the dog eat it*, I thought, as I retched over the kitchen sink.

Jacob imitated my retching. He stood beside me, all two-plus feet of him, and made a gagging noise.

Then, like most mornings that summer, we went outside to shape Play-Doh into letters, his favorite activity.

"C," Jacob requested.

As usual, he wanted letters that are in his name. If I scrambled them, he put them in order. If I gave him enough letters, he'd spell "Mommy," "truck," "blue."

"C is for cookie?" I asked.

He didn't ask for a cookie; serious, he asked for the O.

He was in love with letters and sounds, cracking the code of reading; he was like me, loving words. This thrilled me as much as his exquisitely long eyelashes, the cheeks that tempted the squeezing great-aunt in everybody, the way he adored an ABC book about wildflowers. He ran around the backyard pointing out violet, dandelion, and *Xerophyllum tenax* and then returned to the bench for more letters. He climbed onto my lap as best he could, clearly annoyed by the protrusion of my belly in his way.

"What's in there?" he asked.

"A brother or a sister," I told him. This time we didn't even check at the ultrasound. We liked the surprise. "So you'll be a big brother."

"B," he said. "That spells 'Jacob.'" He held out the Play-Doh. "One," he said, eager to start on the next project, making numbers.

"You can make a one, Tadpole," I said.

Jacob started laughing.

"What is *so* funny?" I asked.

"One," he insisted, proffering green Play-Doh. "Tadpole," he said, and chuckled.

"Is that what you want to name the baby?"

Jacob giggled. He had memorized a book called *Everywhere Babies.* "Everyday everywhere babies are born," he chanted. "Fat babies, fat babies, fat babies." He did not care to repeat the variety in the verse.

"What do you want to name the baby?"

"Tadpole," said Jacob, giggling wildly.

"You want to name the baby Tadpole?"

"Coconut," he said, as if this were obvious. "Coconut, apricot, tadpole."

What beauteous words, I thought. When he finds something hilarious, when he learns something new, it's like whole cities being born.

Now the passion has shifted. Now that he has reached the age where he is allowed to bug us only after his clock reads 6:00, he is in love with math. I knew it was likely he would find pleasure in numbers, but so soon? I don't know when it happened—perhaps when he could read just about everything. We're working with him, during homework time, to match his comprehension with his code-snapping ability to read. But somewhere along the way, numbers usurped letters in his heart.

My husband's family is full of math lovers. His mother, whom I never met, studied math, worked as a statistician for the government. Perhaps I am encountering her through Jacob. My husband studied math in college—math and religion; I studied opera singing and science writing, so we cover as many bases as possible with our early adult passions. Now, of course, we bow to the passions of our children.

I suppose there is a comfort in absolute solutions for Jacob, in right and wrong answers. Especially the right ones. In the car, he plays his Turbo Twist Math games, trying to beat the clock to solve as many problems as he can in . . . sixty seconds! If he's stumped, he yells, "Daddy! What's the answer?" Josh says, "What's the question?" "Ninety minus what equals seventy two?" "It's a building block for algebra," my husband tells me, and he answers.

I don't dislike math, but neither do I love it. In school, I thought the concepts were elegant—the poetic overlapping of universes in logic, for example—but I was never disciplined enough to memorize all the facts you need to manipulate the theory. I made it through to calculus in high school, but I was always struggling in honors classes. My last year of math, I had those dreams in which you are stuffed into a one-piece chair-desk taking an exam and you have no idea how to do what's asked of you. The room is dusty and smells of grape gum. Pencils scratch and no one else is troubled: Even the girl with the Farrah hair in the back row, who hasn't been to class in a month, scribbles away. You are wearing an ill-fitting bikini and there's ice on the floor. You chew your cuticles and hope the answers will magically occur. Okay, I didn't just have those dreams: Except for the bikini and ice, I had those exams.

I'm on the phone with my sister, and our conversation is constantly interrupted; I have to stop to answer, *What's one half of eight? What's six times nine?*—whatever Jacob hasn't memorized yet.

"Soon he'll be ahead of you," she says. And she's right. Sometimes I have to count on my fingers or write it out longhand. A small part of me is always worried my simplest answers will be wrong.

The Den of Math has the following: addition, subtraction, and multiplication cards (he's angling for division, but we're saving that for when he's six); magnetic numbers; the Smath board game; a cash register; a piggy bank; a hundred or so coins; *Mathematickles!*; *Math Fables*; and all those candy-counting and math books you think look dreadful because they'll just make your kid think about eating candy and distract him from the task at hand, but nooo, Jacob loves math more than he loves M&M's. Go figure. It smells of wipe-off marker from his laminated worksheets. There's the sweet smell of boy, too, socks and shampoo, familiar and beloved.

"Why were you up so early?" I ask him.

"Mommy!" he looks up at me, eyes dazzled. "Because I *love* addition. Get the cash register! Make $1.63 using no bills! Buy something!"

I settle on his truck-blanketed bed. Mostly, he just wants an audience.

Though I participate and appreciate, watching him work figures isn't as thrilling for me as watching him teach himself to read. Moreover, math is an interest he primarily shares with his father. There will be other things, but right now this passion aligns daddy and boy—an elemental desire to solve.

"When I grow up," Jacob tells his sister, who herself plans to be a pony, "I'm going to have a job *doing math!*"

At his age, I pretended I had chocolate pudding in my pocket and ate it with an invisible spoon. I made animal parades around the living room, and my sister and I baked a spice cake—no kidding, with all the spices in the rack: cinnamon, cumin, cloves, bay, chili powder, mustard, sweet Hungarian paprika, rosemary, and thyme—as well as the requisite sugar, flour, butter, baking powder, and eggs. Sure, I liked the fact that my last name meant a dozen dozen, but I wasn't learning the rest of the twelve times tables just yet.

I suppose I imagined Jacob's kindergarten connection to his father might be soccer, or Hot Wheels, and although Things Boy were more of a surprise to me than I thought (no interest in the stuffed animals, but those little metal and plastic cars were like talismans, and some vinyl froggies his bedmates), like most parents, I was quick to adapt. But now Jacob is a code cracker, a puzzle solver, and a puzzle at the same time. He will do crosswords, Scrabble, word search, if pressed; but right now he wants what he's so good at—the functions, the question and answer; definitive answers, rather than the subjective work of words. "There were six Cheerios and I ate three!" he exults. "I'm subtracting Cheerios!"

We go to a frozen park in the winter, and he subtracts geese from the shore with a shout. "They're dividing!" he roars, as the flock parts into groups on the icy skin of the water. He wants to estimate, calculate; he loves addends and is starting to ask about exponents. I have to ask my husband for definitions.

Math comes through my son like the genes that make up his beauty: my father's nose and wry smile, my husband's ridiculously long lashes, dark chocolate eyes from at least one great-grandmother. Math comes through him and all else that is to come—he is a boy, he is mine, my husband's, he is his own, and he is surely much greater than the sum of his parts.

Chonan

SUZANNE
KAMATA

The Crown Princess halted nearly all public duties a year ago, apparently due to stress created by pressure to produce a male heir to the throne. Her only child is 3-year-old Princess Aiko, who as a female cannot ascend the Chrysanthemum Throne.
—Japan Times, December 25, 2004

Poor Princess Masako. First, the highly publicized miscarriage, and now she's got shingles because she's under so much stress. The Japanese royal family is the world's oldest continuous monarchy, but she has yet to give birth to the next heir. When royal watchers said that they expected the prince's Harvard-educated bride to transform the monarchy, this wasn't exactly what they had in mind.

Lucky me. I've already produced a son to carry on the Kamata name and bloodline. Although I'm American, not quite the nationality my Japanese in-laws hoped for, there is no nagging about future generations. My daughter, who is deaf and has cerebral palsy, will not be expected to find a husband whom her father and I can adopt, thus insuring we have an heir.

In all honesty, I couldn't care less. I would have been happy with one girl, or all girls, or possibly no children at all, but I am beginning to understand, really understand, what having a son means in Japan.

The day after he was born, his name, Jio, appeared in the newspaper, along with the label *chonan* (eldest son). My daughter Lilia was labeled "eldest daughter," but here, anyway, *chonan* trumps *chojo*. It is the *chonan* who is responsible for taking care of his parents in old age. He is expected to carry on the family farm/take over the family business and to step in as head of the family when his father dies. Later, he's the one who tends the graves of those who've gone on. Other siblings are allowed to work as bartenders, spend years backpacking abroad, or marry into other families and build new houses. A *chonan* never leaves home.

When I tell Japanese women that I married a *chonan*, they nod sympathetically and pat my arm. Before we flew off to Hawaii to exchange vows at the Pua Melia Plantation, I asked, point blank, "Will I have to live with your parents?" Yukiyoshi, my prospective husband, said no, but here we are, twelve years later, preparing to move into his widowed mother's house. (She will be living right next door, in an apartment connected by a corridor.)

My husband's elder sister, the *chojo*, offered to move in with their mother. She, I think, is better qualified for the job, as she speaks Japanese fluently (while I make numerous mistakes and am pretty much illiterate), has teenage able-bodied children, and has actually trained to be a home helper, something my mother-in-law might need several years down the road. But here, on the island of Shikoku, tradition runs deep: My husband has been raised to assume responsibility for his mother (who has a calendar of the imperial family on her wall). Her house, now under renovation, is his birthright.

When Yukiyoshi first laid out his plans to me, he explained that the attached bungalow would be entirely accessible. Although his mother leads an active lifestyle now, he assumes that she will be wheelchair bound, or at least unable to climb a staircase, sooner or later. After she dies, Yukiyoshi explained, Lilia, our disabled daughter, can move in.

We have not yet discussed where he thinks Jio will be living at that time, but it has occurred to me that my husband expects to pass the house on to his son. Jio brings us great joy every day with his big smile, his crazy imagination, his dancing, his baseball hitting, his endless inquiries about Godzilla and the Power Rangers. I, as his American mother, imagine that he will eventually grow up, leave home, and start a family someplace else—maybe even in the United States, which is, after all, his second country. I will be sad for a while, but then I will turn his room into a sewing center, start writing a novel, travel to Africa, and otherwise continue my fabulous life. His father, on the other hand, doesn't seem to believe that he will ever leave. No, Jio will hang out in that small farming community forever, and he and his wife will take care of his sister Lilia, who will be living right next door.

When I was growing up, my parents' relationship was the core bond in our family. I was not allowed to sleep in their bed, ever. My mother and father went on dates and left my brother and me with baby sitters. Later, when I became a difficult adolescent, always at odds with my mother, Dad always sided with Mom. Of course it was understood that my brother and I would eventually leave home, and my parents would remain, together.

When I first got married, I expected the same kind of arrangement. I'd always thought it was a bit weird and sad that mothers often stayed behind with their children when their husbands were transferred to distant cities. I made fun of Japanese mothers' obsessive involvement in their children's lives and the mama's boys who were always hyped in the media. Why, I wondered, did Japanese mothers have to spend every single moment—including nights—with their kids?

However, after my twins were born, my husband and I could hardly bear to sleep apart from them. For their first four years, we slept on four futons laid out in a row. Most of the time, Jio wound up sharing my pillow. And since my husband works up to twelve hours a day, seven days a week (not atypical in Japan), Jio bonded more strongly with me.

We have also bonded through language. Of all the people in our family, Jio is the only one who shares my native tongue. My daughter's first language is Japanese Sign Language, and my husband's is Japanese. My husband communicates with me in English, but only Jio can follow my native-speaker speed. At five, he now knows words that his father doesn't, and I sometimes have to translate for him.

Jio likes to chat in English and to learn new words ("Mommy, what does 'pawpaw patch' mean?"), and he also loves books. My daughter likes looking at the pictures, but she pushes my hands away when I try to sign their meaning. My husband doesn't understand how anyone can get pleasure out of reading books. But Jio comes to me every night at bedtime with a stack of stories. When his *Ladybug* magazine arrives in the mail from America, he literally whoops with joy.

I know that this may change. For the past two years, he has been attending a Japanese preschool, and his Japanese ability has increased daily. These days, if we are in the presence of Japanese speakers—his grandmother, for instance—he tends to address me in Japanese. The words come between us. They push us apart.

It is normal, I know, for him to grow more and more independent, and on one level, I am pleased and amazed to have a bilingual son. But as I watch his attention turn from Madeleine and Babar to Godzilla and Deka Rangers, as he goes deeper into Japanese boy culture, I worry that one day he will refuse to speak English at all. If he rejects my legacy, I will take it personally. I will mourn.

My mother told me recently that I had broken her heart by settling in Japan. When, for a couple of years, my brother lived in Germany, she said that she wished she'd had another child so that one of us would be close to her. She was euphoric when, briefly, my brother and his family lived in the same city and she could see him at least once a week.

My husband was an all-star baseball player in college. He told me once that he'd had a shot at the pros, but his parents summoned him back to Tokushima, where his duties lay, and he became a local high school PE teacher and a baseball coach. His mother has never had her heart broken in the way that mine claims she has.

Although change in Japan occurs at a turtle's pace, the West has influenced Japan. Notions of the nuclear family and individuality have taken root. I've read that living with in-laws is rare in Japan these days, though it's pretty much the norm, for eldest sons' wives anyway, here on the island of Shikoku. Meanwhile, up in Tokyo, the imperial household is considering the possibility of allowing a woman to ascend to the Chrysanthemum throne. (Which would mean that little Aiko would never be able to leave home, palace though it may be.)

Just as American ideas have affected Japan, this country has changed my way of thinking. For example, when I first arrived, I found the tradition of fathers' bathing with small children (especially daughters) unsettling, but now I find it a meaningful ritual. It's one of those rare times in this land of bowing when skin touches skin. Sometimes I spy on the three of them—Yukiyoshi, Jio, and Lilia—in the bath. Lilia laughs when her father sculpts rabbit ears out of shampoo suds, and it was in the bath where Jio learned to count in both Japanese and English, where he tells his father about the incredible feat of eating all his school lunch. And while the thought of seeing my own dad naked kind of creeps me out, I am hopeful that Lilia will grow up with a healthy attitude toward the human body.

Just as my stance on the Japanese bath has changed, my opinions on other aspects of Japanese culture may change in the future. Who knows? Until now, I have believed that it's my job to raise my children to be independent, just as my husband's mother believed, in the Confucian way, hers was to raise her son to be responsible for her. If I start now, I could probably teach my son the same thing. I could conspire to keep him near and spare myself the pain of separation. I could convince him that personal fulfillment is selfish. But I was raised as an American.

Here is where I thank my parents for encouraging my dreams of becoming a writer even though engineering (as suggested by my high school guidance counselor) would have paid better, for allowing me to travel across the ocean, and for supporting my decision to marry the man whom I love even though he lives far away, even though it sometimes makes them sad.

Note to my future self: No matter how much you want to hang on to that boy, you have to let Jio live his own life.

Things You Can't Teach

KATIE
KAPUT

"I'm *so* sorry! He's just so *gentle!*" Or beautiful. Or his hair is *so* long, or he has purple butterfly shoes. Whatever it is this time, other parents at the park make a big show of apologizing for calling my son a girl, all while eyeing me like I may be the source of a virulent infection.

I know what they *want* to ask: "You're a woman in a man's body, right? Like on TV?"

If they asked, and if I felt like answering openly, I could say something like, "I'm a woman in a woman's body! This woman's body just happens to be a little bit different from what you're used to, okay?" I try to jut my chest out a little farther, make it clear that those bumps on my chest are, indeed, small breasts. Having long hair, wearing skirts, and even having breasts can't seem to stop strangers from speculating about whether I'm *really* a man or a woman. I'm always left feeling like there's something wrong with me, even if I can never figure out *what*. If they pushed the "like on TV" angle a bit too forcefully, I'd say, "No, you can't call me a 'she-male.'" I could tell them I call myself a girl or a woman, and that, on the rare occasion that it seems relevant in my day-to-day life, I might preface "girl" with "transsexual."

But then they'd just say, "So you're a woman in a man's body, right?" and we'd be back where we started.

I've been answering questions like those since I had the misfortune of being a freshman in high school and coming out as a transsexual girl, all in one year. Questions don't bother me. Questions are easy to handle compared to the shame, the isolation, and the violence I've experienced being a girl with a "different" kind of girl's body, a body most people still seem to see as a "boy's body." Most people forget that if I had a boy's body, I'd be a boy. I'm a girl, and, regardless of my discomfort with parts of it, my body *is* a girl's body. Still, on most days I can answer even the rudest questions about myself. But I'm struggling for the answers when it comes to raising my son.

I'd always thought I would have a daughter, right up until the moment when the ultrasound technician told us otherwise. After all, I was contributing my transsexual girl's egg (okay, call it sperm if you absolutely must, but you'd better be a medical professional) to my partner's egg, and an egg plus an egg equals, well, another egg, right? A girl.

But Rio was a little baby boy.

I tried not to worry about it, but sometimes when I was folding the blue truck-emblazoned onesies everyone kept giving us after he was born, I wondered if I could possibly handle the pressures of raising a boy.

I had *hated* being forced to play with trucks and baseballs when I was little, and I chafed against the ridiculous manly boy outfits my parents found for me in their quest to reinforce my masculinity. I had firsthand experience being force-fed boyhood, and it had taken years of surrounding myself with other girls and submerging myself in girl-affirming art and culture for me to stop feeling like a tomato plant dropped in the shade of a house in the Midwest in midwinter: misplaced, cared for improperly, *dying*.

I didn't want that experience for Rio, whether he was going to be masculine or feminine, boy or girl (or some other interesting combination of those options).

But if he *did* like "girly" things, would everyone accuse me of brainwashing him? Preventing him from achieving a normal level of masculinity? After all, maybe they'd think it was all because I lusted after tiny pony dolls with real pink hair requiring thrice-daily brushing that he ended up, you know, light in the diapers.

"He's three months old," pointed out a well-meaning but unhelpful and childless friend.

"I wouldn't be worrying about it if I wasn't so goddamn *queer!*" I whined. "Straight parents don't have to worry about this stuff: If their kid jumps the fence and gets into the dolls, the worst anyone can say about them is that they let it happen! But if mine puts on the high heels, who do you think they're gonna come looking for?"

"Just who is this 'they' coming to look for you?" my friend asked.

Paranoia aside, at the park, under the watchful eyes of a dozen or more presumably straight middle-aged parents, it can feel as though my very existence as a transsexual mama is a giant visual aid placed in Rio's constant view by the Campaign to Create More Transsexual Girls, or At Least Sissy Boys.

The thing is, Rio liked his "boyish" toys and clothes well enough (although *of course* I resisted and resented the gendered toy terminology), but as he grew and started crawling and then walking, he also liked to play with little pink balls of cotton fluff, remnants of a craft kit I'd long ago borrowed from my little sister, that he'd find on the floor. When he started talking and was able to pick his own clothes, one of his first purchases was a pair of pink pants.

Nothing to worry about, right? And even if this interest in pink did imply anything about his future gender and sexuality, who cares, right? It's okay to be gay (or even trans), and some of us, at least, are born that way.

Easy for everyone else to say.

I'm being observed by hordes of potential gender enforcers on a daily basis.

If Rio happens to be at the park wearing a barrette, I can just imagine someone assuming that was my choice and not his. I can imagine someone assuming I'm pushing this queer thing a bit too hard. As if I even *wore* barrettes. Because isn't it a slippery slope? Aren't barrettes a gateway accessory, leading ever onward to queerer and queerer fashion decisions? One day, little boys who wear barrettes could end up passed out on the floor of their messy teenage bedrooms in a sea of hair clippers and nail polish, endlessly pondering the question, "Buzz my head, or paint my nails . . . ?"

Dealing with this gender judgment has been difficult. I have tried taking deep breaths. I have told myself that, at the very least, my family and my partner's family and all of our friends have been supportive of Rio's playing with whatever he wants and being whoever he is going to be. I have reminded myself it really *is* okay to be gay or trans in our chosen community, even if it isn't in most communities.

But still it has been hard. I was so worried that other people would judge me unfit to be a parent because I was a transsexual girl that I drove myself mad. Friends assured me they couldn't tell I was upset, but at my worst in wrestling with parenting a boy, I was flailing. I couldn't figure out where my loyalties should lie: with the coercive and cruel larger society or with my own supportive community, a community of queers, grrrls, transpeople, and our families and friends.

The problem was, my community was stretched thin by geographical distance. At a time I needed my friends the most, I was far away from them. I had been active in a Riot Grrrl chapter and a Lesbian Avengers group, but that was in Chicago. Palo Alto, California, where I live now, is a long way from there. Besides, my friends have always been the stay-up-late, wake-up-late sort, and Rio has always been the bed-at–5 PM wake-up-at–5 AM sort, which made even phone calls difficult to schedule for a time when my friends and I were both awake.

Rio was unaware of my turmoil. He was happy with all of it—his little pink balls of fluff, his pink pants, his blue t-shirt, his trucks. Rio, far from being an empty vessel for my unintentional brainwashing vibes, was his own little guy.

The rapid growth of his ability to express himself really turned things around for me. Now it's obvious to me that he has all his own likes and dislikes that are beyond my control, and even, to some extent, beyond my influence. He's interested in things no one in his immediate circle of friends and family had any interest in before he showed us the wonder of them: car models; telling stories about "a red truck, a blue truck, two pink trucks, and a purple truck"; and eating orange peels.

I didn't teach him to play with pink balls of fluff or trucks. He was just exploring. He was just being a kid, checking out different colors and textures. If he waited for me to show him everything, he would hardly have gotten around to discovering fluff trucks or a million other things he knows deeply, whether gender-normative or not.

I seem to be getting good at playing with dump trucks full of pink balls of fluff; at least, Rio seems to like it when I drive them around and make obnoxious engine noises. The trucks have become fun for me, and as for his wardrobe, he looks really cute in all kinds of clothes, pink, blue, or otherwise, because, well, he just *is* cute. He's a toddler heartthrob, no doubt about it, no matter which way you like your cute tiny kids. I've realized through my own parenting that my favorite kind of cute tiny kid is the kind who's given lots of freedom to decide how to look and how to spend time.

There's still a struggle in me sometimes, between a part of me that wants him to be like me—be a miniature me, not in the sense of being trans or queer, but in the sense of loving things I love and valuing things I value—and a part of me that has grown into an awareness that my son's interests will interest me no matter what. A part of me that is ready to really love trucks and baseball for the joy they bring him, if trucks and baseball are what bring him joy.

Statistically, it's unlikely that he'll turn out to be trans, or even queer; but if he does, he'll be one of the lucky ones, because he'll have a mother who knows a lot about being that kind of kid. But whoever he turns out to be, I am learning a lot about raising the kind of kid he already is: free spirited, intelligent, expressive, sensitive. If I can just turn down the volume on my own paranoia and turn up the volume on the trucks full of fluff, I'll do a good job supporting him in being whoever he turns out to be.

That *is* the whole point, after all.

Scaredy-Cat

JODI
PICOULT

At first, I blamed Frank and Joe.

You know—the Hardy Boys. Far from being the clean-cut twosome that's entertained a few generations of young people, discerning readers realize that those two are Evil Incarnate. Or, rather, they stumble upon Evil Incarnate every now and then, which is enough to unsettle fans who aren't, well, quite as Hardy. Case in point: The bedroom door cracked open—for the third time that night—and Kyle, my eleven-year-old, stood restlessly in the slice of light in the hallway. "I still can't get it out of my mind," he whispered.

Beside me, my husband groaned. My husband, the one who got up all night without complaint each time we had an infant in the house. But then, a repeated lack of sleep would probably make even Mother Teresa cranky. "Go to bed," he grunted. "Again."

"I just want to know if you'll throw this out." Kyle tossed his new Hardy Boys chapter book on the bed as if it harbored the plague. "I don't like knowing it's in my room."

165

"This?" I asked, sitting up. "The book you begged me to buy you? The one you couldn't stop talking about at dinner, because of the way they found the gold treasure?"

Kyle took a step inside, checking over his shoulder in the hall . . . *for what?* I wondered. Ghosts? Goblins? Siblings? "The thing is, on page 214, they see a skeleton in the back of the cave. And . . . I can't get it out of my head."

We did our old song and dance: The skeleton is part of a story; stories can't hurt you. Sniffling, Kyle went back to his room, turned on enough lights to illuminate Fenway Park, and blasted country music on his radio. I heard him hiccupping for a few more minutes . . . then, quiet. Closing my eyes, I lay back and pulled up the covers.

The door swung open again. "Mom? Is there any chance we could make a fire right now and burn it?"

I am the mother of a scaredy-cat. Kyle, at age eleven, has not outgrown the fears that terrify younger children. In fact, now that he's developed the mental capability to justify to himself why something might be stalking the woods behind our home, or why it's possible that the thump he heard downstairs is a burglar, it's even tougher. I should have known. When Kyle was little and we went to a playgroup, the other mothers would tell horror stories of their boys climbing draperies or freeing the guinea pig. Kyle, on the other hand, was certain the bogeyman was hiding in the drapery folds; he would never free the guinea pig, because rodents might bite. When we went for our flu shots, it took three oversize residents to hold Kyle down. He would close his eyes tight when we drove by a graveyard; he needed not one night-light, but two.

My younger kids are nothing like Kyle. Jake, his nine-year-old brother, lets the world roll right off his shoulders. Even things that should have scared him—for example, repeat surgeries for an inner ear disorder—didn't merit more than a shrug. Instead, *Kyle* asked a thousand questions at the dinner table about how much blood there would be and if the stitches would look like the Frankenstein monster's. Likewise, Kyle's seven-year-old sister is forty pounds of empowerment. Sammy has been known to deck boys who bother her on the bus. At night she waits until Kyle dozes off, then creeps into the hall and shuts off all the lights he's turned on, so that she can finally fall asleep.

I assumed that Kyle would outgrow his anxieties, the same way he lost the dubious gift of being able to stick objects of all shapes and sizes up his nose. But he learned to read, took one look at a headline, and asked if we have tornadoes in New Hampshire. He systematically removed every video from the video shelf that had objectionable scary scenes, in his opinion, and squirreled them away until his siblings discovered what he was doing. "Mom," Jake complained, "how could *Alice in Wonderland* be scary?"

"The Cheshire cat," Kyle muttered. "It freaks me out."

Well, the Cheshire cat kind of freaks me out too, come to think of it. But *Charlotte's Web?*

"Mom! Wilbur almost gets killed in it!"

"But he *doesn't*," I pointed out.

"So?" Kyle scoffed. "He *could*."

And that is the root of my son's problem. His imagination—that immeasurable spark that makes him a superb artist, a fabulous storyteller, and a very cool playmate at recess—runs away with him. During the day, imagination is the most wonderful part of him; at night, it is the bane of his existence. Happy endings can be erased with a "what if"; logic pales in comparison to the tales of possibility he weaves in his own mind. What Kyle is afraid of, really, is the power of his own mind.

Before 9/11, I had a much better handle on parenting. I knew what was safe and what wasn't; I could say with conviction that planes did not fall out of the sky on purpose; I believed that children you tucked in at night were secure in their bedrooms. I worried on my children's behalf about bullies and cliques and the day the cafeteria served fun fish shapes for lunch—not about anthrax and smallpox and wars half a world away.

After 9/11, however, I got scared. I remember taking the kids to school, where Kyle turned to me before getting out of the van. "Mom," he asked, "is anything going to happen to us here?"

"No," I heard myself tell him firmly, although my hands were shaking. "We're all going to be fine."

That's the other thing that happened after 9/11—I found myself lying to my own children. I told them they were safe, when the truth was, I really wasn't entirely sure. I hoped, like everyone else, and gradually, I stopped worrying and started to live my life. Maybe I spent an extra minute kissing my kids goodnight, or looked back one extra time in the rearview mirror while we were driving . . . but I learned to live in the present, instead of the possible. In short, I made myself take the advice I'd been giving Kyle all these years.

If you've got a fear, there's a name for it. *Paraskavedekatriaphobia:* fear of Friday the thirteenth. *Arachibutyrophobia:* fear of peanut butter sticking to the roof of one's mouth. *Alektrophobia:* fear of chickens. Some fears are groundless, and some are painfully based in reality. But kids aren't the only ones who suffer—which of us adults wouldn't admit to a slight *rhytiphobia* (fear of getting wrinkles)? What is a midlife crisis, really, but a slight *atychiphobia* (fear of failure)? Part of growing up means realizing that we aren't perfect (*atelophobia*: fear of imperfection). The question is, should our fears grow up with us?

When I was a kid, my younger brother used to twist himself into knots every morning before he went to school. Today, he's the youngest senior vice president at his Fortune 500 company: He gets paid a great deal of money to worry on behalf of thousands of employees. Maybe a little worry is a good thing. Maybe nervousness is the twin sister of awareness, a seed that blooms into self-responsibility, social consciousness, and vigilance.

The world is not the sparkling wonderland we like to imagine it is for the sake of our offspring—we know now, more than ever, that it's a scary, uncertain place. As parents, we hope we have the power to keep our children from growing up enough to understand this. It is devastating for me to watch Kyle when he's terrified of something because it reminds me what I'm most terrified of: my own failure to keep him safe. I've known all along that one day the child who considered me his protector was going to find out I was not invincible. What happens when Kyle realizes that a mom is not a hero, but just a person who, like him, can be kept awake at night by her own fears?

Recently, Kyle had a homework assignment for English, to graph the best and worst moments of his life. Some peaks and valleys I expected: the day his grandmother died, the joyous trips to Arizona, his first eagerly anticipated piano lesson. Others were more surprising: a fight with a friend that apparently was far more devastating than I'd thought; losing a Game Boy cartridge. And there, graphed nearly at the all-time nadir of the dog being hit by a car, was 9/11.

I asked him about it. "How come you put that down as one of your worsts?"

"Because," Kyle said, "I didn't know what else was going to happen."

I'd like to believe that a parent's job is to protect, but not to pretend. A child who feels safe is more likely to take risks. A child who knows he'll be looked after is more likely to explore. Yet maybe it's all right to admit that grownups have bogeymen, too; that there are things running through our heads at night that make it hard to fall asleep. Maybe we can show kids that being brave doesn't always come easily to us, either. Maybe we can be our children's safety net, and they can be ours.

And maybe we can remember that very few of us are *pantophobic*— that is, afraid of everything. The girl who panics around a mouse you think is kind of cute might be the one who crushes a spider that's got you paralyzed with fear. Sometimes we are so wrapped up in the situations that terrify us, it's easy to forget there are situations where our courage shines.

This fall, we took a family trip to a nearby alpine slide—a fun day, to be certain, for someone who's not terrified of heights. As I stood at the base of the chairlift with my family scowling at me, Kyle stepped forward and took my hand. "I'll help you, Mom," he said, and he did: telling me just where to stand when the bench swept us up from behind, lowering the safety bar by himself when my hands were paralyzed, talking to me to keep my mind off the scenery scrolling so very, very far beneath us. "You okay?" Kyle asked. I nodded, took a deep breath. I told myself, like a mantra, that I could do this. I could spit right in the eye of my fear, and laugh.

Kyle interrupted my reverie. "Hey, Mom?" he asked. "What's a mausoleum?"

The Velvet Underground

SUSAN
O'DOHERTY

In 1969, at the height of the Vietnam War, a war broke out in my house between my father and brother. The disputed offense was the perceived sissiness of my brother, who had quit playing football, taken up the guitar, and grown his hair long. The climactic battle took place the night my brother appeared at the dinner table sporting a softball-sized peace medallion on what looked like a bicycle chain. My father, purple with Seagram's-fueled rage, shouted that no son of his was going to prance around in a necklace and, when my brother refused to remove it, took a swing at him. Belying the purported message of his "necklace," my brother pushed my father, with force, up against the dining room wall, then stomped up to his room. A few minutes later, Lou Reed's voice came blasting down the stairs, assaulting our ears with disclosures about the varieties of love.

I remained at the table, shaking. I would like to claim that my distress was based on an abhorrence of violence and a concern for the physical and emotional well-being of my family, but this was not the case. I had been weaned on oral pugilism, and my dad had never hesitated to resort to manual reinforcement when words failed. This was the first time my brother had struck back, but my primary response to that gesture was a sense of liberation, mingled with guilty relief that I wasn't the one who was in for it. No, what struck me so forcefully was the belated realization (this was, after all, six years after the publication of *The Feminine Mystique*) that the attributes my father was condemning as "sissy" were, in fact, those traits that were characteristic of girls, or at least were encouraged in girls: softness, vulnerability, and a taste for personal adornment. If these qualities were so contemptible as to incite a fistfight, what did that say about me, about any hope I had to be a serious participant in the world at large?

This question was, of course, not original to me. It has plagued, informed, and prodded generations of women in their work and family lives. That evening, though, while my father and brother struck each other, I was struck by the realization that the frilly dresses and Suzy Homemaker kits that had been the prizes of my childhood (and had evolved into floral granny gowns and the privilege of baking organic ten-grain bread for my poet boyfriend) were in fact instruments of irrelevance, if not degradation.

Since that night, I have devoted a great deal of psychic energy to sorting out which elements of my "basic girl training" are valuable (interpersonal sensitivity, love of beauty, an appreciation of the essentials of nutrition and hygiene) and which deserve to be trashed (my difficulty in taking seriously anyone who arrives at an important meeting in a pink lace blouse, my sense that if my shoes are comfortable, I'm probably underdressed). Is my habitual conversational sarcasm a destructive artifact of my combative childhood, or a healthy response to nonsense; does it feel wrong to me because it is potentially hurtful, or because it runs counter to the sugar-and-spice ideal?

I did not fully grasp the extent to which my father and brother were also gender war losers, though, until the morning the Battle of the Dining Room was reenacted inside my head when my three-year-old son, Ben, announced his plan to wear "the fancy ones" to preschool.

By "the fancy ones" he meant a gaudy costume jewelry ensemble I'd received as a gift. I would have donated it to Goodwill long before had Ben not fallen under the spell of the sparkly faux gold, amethyst, and ruby necklace and clip-on earrings. He was in the habit of parading around our apartment sporting a chiffon scarf, my patent-leather pumps, and the fancy ones, as his father and I oohed in admiration. Ben's assumption that the world at large would similarly embrace his elegance was not surprising, but I hadn't anticipated that he would test it out.

You may think, as I did for many years, that the dining room encounter between my father and brother had little to do with any kind of love, Lou Reed notwithstanding. Parenting a boy has forced me to reconsider this assumption. My father was one of nine children growing up in an Irish immigrant family in a rough section of the Bronx. Boys were expected to defend themselves with their fists, their feet, and, if necessary, weapons. His younger brother, a shy, lisping cherub, was ambushed and abducted on his way home from Catholic school by a rival group of public school boys and held over a trash can fire until blisters erupted on his feet and legs. In my father's universe, a longhaired, bejeweled boy might as well wear a sign reading, COME AND GET ME. His continual efforts to toughen my brother up—to make a man out of him—were, in part, attempts to shield my brother from the consequences of exposing his tenderness to a brutal world.

Only in part, though, and at tremendous cost. My father's own youthful enjoyment of romantic opera and Victorian novels had been pushed underground early on, to emerge only at the maudlin ends of drunken evenings. He and my brother related to one another as wary adversaries, their love (not that they would tolerate the word) expressed primarily through a shared appreciation of spectator sports and Marx Brothers movies. My father suffered for years with hypertension, which we didn't need a cardiologist to tell us was exacerbated by his chronic anger and inability to admit to sadness, helplessness, or vulnerability.

I was aware of all this when Ben made his sartorial pronouncement. I had sworn that my son was going to be raised differently, with a healthy appreciation for the softer, more traditionally feminine side of life. I had explained, patiently, to my parents and interested neighbors that we were glad he liked to play with his baby doll, that boys as well as girls benefit from parenting practice. I was aware that the assignation of "femininity" to a particular color or type of adornment is arbitrary and has varied widely over the centuries and across continents. And I was certain that in the twenty-five years since the confrontation in my parents' dining room, society had developed some tolerance for gender ambiguity.

On the other hand, I had recently returned to work as a psychologist at an inner-city elementary school where apprentice gang members routinely beat up boys they considered "wimps" or "faggots," and where the teachers considered banishment to the girls' recess line an appropriate punishment for misbehaving boys. When Ben was six months old, the teacher of a "gymnastics class" I had enrolled him in as a vehicle for meeting other parents warned me, in complete seriousness, that he was in danger of becoming a "mama's boy" if I continued to pick him up whenever he cried. And of course I carried the memory of my father's protective rage.

And so, that morning, when Ben asked me if he could wear the fancy ones to school, I hesitated, long enough to communicate to him that something was amiss in his request. "I won't lose them," he promised.

I explained that some people didn't think boys should wear necklaces and that they might say "mean things" to him. After some deliberation, he decided to take the risk, and so we set off.

In the elevator of our apartment building, a neighbor—an attorney with whom we had exchanged friendly small talk for years—stared in obvious confusion at this child arrayed in worn jeans, a Knicks t-shirt, Hot Wheels sneakers, and the fancy ones. As we emerged in the lobby, the neighbor commented, "All this time, I thought she was a boy!" On the street, another acquaintance admonished me, "What are you trying to do, turn him into a girl?" And we were greeted at the door to his classroom by a female classmate who demanded, "Don't you know boys aren't supposed to wear earrings?" Both Ben's teacher and I intervened immediately, explaining that in fact many men and boys do wear earrings, and in any case, this was a "safe place" for children to dress any way they chose. It was too late, though. Ben removed the offending articles and slunk into a corner of the classroom, buried his head in his hands, and refused all overtures of encouragement or comfort. He never donned the fancy ones again.

When he was in kindergarten, Ben rescued an outworn embroidered-velvet evening jacket from the Goodwill pile "because it's so soft and beautiful." However, he said, he intended to hide it at the bottom of his shirt drawer. "It would be too embarrassing if anyone saw it," he informed me.

Last year, a schoolmate left her pink, Barbie-emblazoned backpack behind at an event we attended, and I suggested that Ben return it to her at school the next day. He refused to touch it. After some negotiation, he agreed to let me carry it to school on the condition that I keep it wrapped in a brown paper bag, so that none of his friends could possibly see it and connect it with him in any way.

What happens to the tenderness, the love of beauty, the softness that we continue to discourage in boys in so many overt and subtle ways? Typically, traits that we deem unacceptable in ourselves are first pushed underground, like Ben's velvet jacket; then disowned, like his schoolmate's Barbie backpack; and finally done away with, either symbolically or, too often, literally. I now work at a counseling center that serves victims of domestic violence, and I am increasingly convinced that the perpetrators we excoriate as brutal predators are themselves victims who have internalized all too well our culture's message that vulnerability, and those who embody it, are worthy of contempt and abuse. Moreover, it seems clear that the planet is imperiled primarily because so many world leaders have been trained, like my father, to respond to any threat—of attack from the outside, or of sadness, weakness, or delicacy from inside themselves—with anger, posturing, and retaliation.

At age ten, Ben is an ardent and competitive athlete. He has explained to me that one reason he enjoys playing the drums at school events is that "it feels so good to hit things." I am no longer allowed to kiss or hug him in front of his friends. I imagine my dad beaming down approvingly from whichever celestial pub he's assigned to, saying, "You've got yourself a real buster there." My husband and I alternate between admiring Ben's considerable strengths and worrying about where they will take him, always seeking that elusive balance between cultivating his more sensitive, vulnerable side—his fancy ones—and ensuring that his COME AND GET ME sign is not legible to any and all.

And of course I take it all personally. The openhearted love and admiration he expressed as a little boy, the love that warmed and sustained me, is now being pushed underground; and I can't escape the fear that I, too, will be disowned and discarded. How much of this is a natural, even desirable, developmental process and how much a response to our culture's continued hostility toward "wimpiness" remains an open and problematic question.

And yet: Last spring, after hearing a cellist friend play in a series of concerts, Ben became interested in studying the cello. Already his teacher and others have remarked on the sensitivity of his fingering and the beauty of his tones. Recently he decided that I need to learn as well, "so we can play duets." He is a gentle and encouraging teacher, patiently molding my stiff, middle-aged fingers around the bow; showing me over and over again movements that he picked up easily the first time; and ending each lesson with the assurance, "You're doing great. Really." My brother now has three boys of his own who are growing into creative, responsible, and loving young men. And when I broached the topic of this essay with Ben, concerned that he might be embarrassed by the revelations that he had worn a necklace to preschool and fallen in love with a velvet jacket, he encouraged me to write it, "to let people know it's not fair that boys aren't allowed to do girl things without being laughed at."

So I'm telling you. As Lou Reed might say, maybe we are beginning to see the light.

Pretty Baby

CATHERINE
NEWMAN

Was that you, sitting behind us at *The Nutcracker on Ice?* Remember? Your kid was tangled up in her own scarf and then weeping over a box of spilled raisins before she peed "one tiny, tiny drop" into her tights? But still you could hear our Ben's sharp intake of breath when the skaters all glided out in pairs. You heard his whispery loud "That's so beautiful!" about their powdered white wigs and spingly-spangly outfits, real pretend snow fluttering around them as they twirled their romantic figure eights. Oh, those fancy parents of the *Nutcracker* children! Those mothers skating around in fitted pink-satin waistcoats and full pink-satin skirts, those fathers just barely distinct in their own cotton candy waistcoats, although they weren't wearing skirts, of course—I mean, it wasn't *Nutcracker on Castro Street*, for God's sake. No, the fathers were sporting the super-manly pink-satin knickers. And Ben loved them.

Later, when we were zipping up our jackets in the lobby—after the scuffling soldier mice and the various Freudian dream sequences of hunky toys that may or may not come to life and look like a person's dad, after the

"Dance of the Sugar Plum Fairy" and Ben's baby sister falling asleep in my lap like a thirty-pound sack of sausages—Ben identified "that pink part" as the very best segment of the entire evening.

I was not surprised. Ben is five, and pink has always been his favorite color. Just to be clear, we're not talking *pale* pink—which he will tolerate but has no special affinity for (it ranks seventh on his list, behind even *teal*)—but bright pink, or what he sometimes calls "darky pink." When, for instance, I wore my reversible down jacket with the black side out, he thought I was insane. "If I had all that nice darky pink in my coat, I would definitely show it." (He had a point. I reversed it.) His own jacket is silver, but his snow boots are flamingo pink, as is the fraying plastic lei from a midwinter luau. His favorite flowers are pink roses. And his most special outfit—the one he wears only for such extraordinary occasions as a birthday party or the weekly show-and-tell at his preschool—involves a floral-printed t-shirt with fuchsia velour sleeves, and the pants that I myself made (with much saying of the F-word and sewing of my actual hand to the fabric) from the magenta-striped terry cloth that Ben picked out from Jo-Ann Fabrics.

Right about now you're probably sending enthusiastic "You go, boy!" vibes in Ben's direction—and you should be. For one thing, he looks absolutely fabulous. And for another, maybe pink is the new navy blue. After all, P. Diddy swaggers in sweatpants the color of a seashell, and Demi Moore ogles her young hottie in his taffy-hued suit. Briefcase-carrying hominids seem to have worn sherbety-pink shirts beneath their ties since the Dawn of Business Attire. And yet the color rules are different for little boys. Is that because we imagine a grown man's gender is already hardened and set, like the steely abdomen of masculinity itself, the threat of pink bouncing off it like so many girly punches? While evidently for budding young manhood—the preschool type—pink must be shunned like gender-bending kryptonite. Like it's some queer wolf in powdery-pale clothing. Pink might *seem* to be a swishy little color—but it's got the strength of entire armies. Why, merely gazing too long at a carnation could prevent your son's very testicles from descending! And forget the actual *wearing* of the color—that could send his Y chromosomes leaping for their lives onto the nearest testosterone-leaking Arnold Schwarzenegger look-alike.

I know this must be true, because I write an online parenting column, and whenever I post a picture of Ben in this or that pink outfit—or with the rolling pink Hello Kitty suitcase he wanted (and got) for his fourth birthday—the message boards fill with enraged, apocalyptic postings about our family's imminent nellification. "Why is your son wearing pink?" is what people want to know—although they don't tend to ask quite so politely. (And you'd be surprised at how unsatisfactory they find the perfectly logical answer "Because pink is his favorite color.") From the shrillness of their indignation, you'd think we were taking Ben back-to-school shopping at Frederick's of Hollywood instead of Old Navy, which is where we actually go (when we're not at the Salvation Army).

And all I'll say is, you try convincing a young child to choose from the racks of boy clothes. Do we really expect boys to thrill to one of those midget salesmen outfits—the tomato-red polo shirts and pleated khaki slacks—or over an oatmeal-colored sweater vest and army-green camouflage sweatpants? Are we genuinely shocked that the girls' section—with its plush bubblegum everything, its rhinestones and puppies and velvet detailing—calls out to some boys like a pastel siren song? Of course not. But even when nobody says it outright, we know what the critics are thinking: Let your son wear pink, and you might as well enroll him in Camp Fire Island. Because pink isn't just nouveau Hollywood-hip and retro neo-preppy golf sweaters. It's still totally Elton John and Village People. It still means taking out a lease in Gayville—with an option to buy.

Yes, nobody likes to come right out and say it (actually, plenty do), but that's what all of this is about. Everyone wants to be sure that, a dozen years from now, our sons will have the right kind of prom date—the *vagina* kind of prom date. Which they surely won't, unless we police their color choices a little more rigorously. But here's where I get confused—simple pinheaded bigotry aside. If "pink" and "gay" go together like Froot Loops and Toucan Sam, is pink imagined to be the *effect* of gayness? Or its cause? Because if it's the former—if pink is the mere expression of some extant *essential* gayness—well then, what's the point of worrying about it? It's a fait accompli, so pour me a glass of champagne, pop in a Barbra Streisand movie, and let's celebrate. But if it's taken instead to be the cause, then how, exactly *does* pink make a boy gay? Does he grow up to be a pink-wearing adult, at which point other men—woops!—mistake him for a Victoria's Secret model and hit on him by accident and, well, one thing leads to another, when in Rome, etc.? Or do the color waves actually alter his brain chemistry such that his ideal wife spontaneously becomes Tom Selleck?

For one thing: I doubt it. And for another: Great—even if it's not Tom Selleck. I'll be delighted. (Wouldn't you much rather, for instance, that your son be *shacked up* with the Queer Eye Fab Five than waiting shlubbily for them to come and fix him?)

Or is the worry just that pink will keep Ben from achieving his proper patriarchal birthright? *Oh masculinity! So natural and true! As teetering and precarious as an ice-fishing house built from fairy wings!* Will Ben's preschool class photo be uncovered one day and threaten his entry into the World Wrestling Federation? Will those pink-threaded boyhood outfits prevent him from registering a firearm or sucking beer out of somebody's ass crack at a fraternity hazing? Will he be clinically incapable of slouching in front of the Super Bowl like an overgrown, chili-fed larva? Or do we just worry that he won't know how to camouflage himself properly as an *imbecile stone* when a lover tries to enter together with him into the world of human feelings? I mean, men are great and everything—my own dearly beloved is a man, for example—but the last time I checked, gender roles didn't seem to be working so well for everyone. Why would we take such good care of something that seems to make so many people—gay and straight, men and women—so unhappy? And why on earth would we start so young?

Or younger. Because even when Ben was a mere wisp of a newborn, boyness seemed to cast its peculiar blue shadow over him. Our best friends had had a baby before us, and Ben wore her hand-me-down onesies and rompers, all of them decorated variously with whimsical fruits and zoo animals. Nothing was frilly or girly or even pink, but because these were not typical boy-baby clothes—insofar as they were without the obligatory decals of footballs and bulldozers and naked women—Ben was often mistaken for a girl. Which was fine with us—I mean, it wasn't like we needed him to hop up and carve our Thanksgiving turkey or anything. He was only fifteen seconds old, after all. But people would gush over him—"Oh what a pretty baby! Oh she's gorgeous!"—and we would beam and nod until the moment they asked "her" name, when we would have to confess, "Well, actually, it's Ben." And then his admirer would fall into fits of apology. "Oh my God! I'm so sorry! I don't know how I missed it! I mean, now that I really look—he's so handsome. So *manly.*" Even though little Ben would just be dozing neutrally in the front pack, with his rosebud lips and male pattern baldness. It wasn't like he was cruising for a fiancé. "Oh that's okay," we always said. "We don't care!"

And we didn't. Or at least not about that. Because we *do* care—so much that it's like an ache at the bottom of my throat—about other things. Like Ben's happiness. His wholeness. We want him to be himself, to do the things he likes—however contradictory these things may be. Like the time he was two, and he toddled into the living room with a beaded pink-and-orange evening bag slung elegantly over his shoulder—then turned it over and dumped out a heap of Matchbox cars, *vroomed* them around like a maniac. Or the summer he wore the t-shirt our artist friend Meg made him: a little pink scoop-neck with the word "boy" silk-screened in black. He loves glittery purple eye shadow (which he applies only to the groove between his nose and mouth) and his iridescent strawberry-kiwi Bonne Bell Lipsmacker—and also running around, yelling, with a plastic baseball bat stuck out from between his legs. He loves his stuffed Snow Bear so tenderly that his eyes glisten while he cuddles her—but play the associations game with him, and the prompt "boring" will cause him to spit out the words "baby doll" like so much chewed-up tobacco.

Ben wants to decorate his birthday cake with rose petals and also gummy worms. He covets (and wears) bejeweled hair accessories although his hair is cut short, and he loves stringing glass beads and setting up elaborate tracks for his trains. His very best friend is a girl, but his second- and third-best friends are both boys. He likes to arrange the pansies and bleeding hearts in his grandmother's flower press. Dinosaurs scare him. He's a fearless climber. He recently told me that he thinks he's a fan of the Red Sox, "but," he admitted, "only because of the word "socks"—not because of how they play that game." He's happy and funny and smart. And he's very kind.

Which may be why, at *The Nutcracker*, after we'd gathered up all our mittens and scarves and Ben was twirling merrily toward the exit in blue racing-stripe sweatpants and a pink shirt with a heart on its sleeve, you leaned over your sleeping daughter and whispered to me, "Your son is lovely." And my eyes filled with tears—I could only smile and nod—because it's true. He is. And it was lovely of you to notice.

Our Bodies, Their Selves

MARION
WINIK

There are days when the only reason I love my children is because they're so unbelievably good-looking. That honey-colored hair. The curve of that baby belly. The wholly innocent lower lip. Those round, clear eyes with their pale fringe of lashes. Sometimes a sweet little bare foot, perhaps with a 101 Dalmatians Band-Aid on the fourth toe, can almost make up for two hours of whining and a puddle of Gatorade. I often answer the question "How are your boys?" with "They're adorable." Well, they are.

I love my children's bodies, and they love mine. Of course we feel this way: We used to be one. In the beginning, they popped right out of me and amazed me with their loveliness, their soft hair, their tiny hands, their midnight-blue eyes—and their fingertip-size penises and swollen purple testicles, which to this day I have trouble believing were manufactured here in Marion's womb. As if their beauty alone might not be enough to win me over, there was the sheer physical delight of taking care of them, of cuddling and carrying and cradling,

189

of relearning the parts of my own body in motherly terms. These breasts, these hips, this lap—now I get it! Equipment!

I was a passionate breastfeeder from day one. It enthralled me that my body had the power to sustain another life. Nursing was so clearly a sensual experience that I joked about how fast my infant sons could get my bra off, and speculated as to how my nursing unabashed in virtually every environment and position would play out in their postpubescent futures. No matter how I joked, I never felt weird about it. I knew that you can't hold a baby too long, or kiss his toes too often. The fact that I enjoyed it so much was wired into me for the perpetuation of the species.

Oh, that seems like a long time ago. Though I still love to hug and kiss my big third grader and his younger brother, it's getting hard to believe I used to stick a breast in their mouths. And after years of bathing, dressing, and sleeping with them, and parading around the house in the nude (as I have been prone to do all my life), I'm starting to feel a little shy. As young as they are, the first green shoots of sexuality began to germinate some time ago, and I have to be careful about the role that my body—the opposite sex in its inaugural incarnation—plays in their development.

Our gradual loss of innocence seems to have begun as far back as the day I stopped nursing. When Hayes, at eighteen months, would tackle me; push up my shirt; and storm my brassiere, often biting me with his new set of teeth, I began to feel sort of violated. I remembered the good old days when my breasts were my sole and private property: nonfunctional, eroticized, never on view to strangers in restaurants. Enough with the udders. I wanted my pointless breasts back. Yet while I was suddenly over nursing, I wasn't ready to relinquish the comfort we got from the touch of each other's skin.

Through Hayes's kindergarten year, we still took baths together, slipping and sliding around the soapy tub. At night, both of them would toddle, later tiptoe, into my bed, clinging like barnacles to the mamaboat until dawn. I had mixed feelings about this practice, as Vincie had the habit of wrapping his little hands around my neck, rhythmically clutching and unclutching, and Hayes would often wake me with a hot stream of pee. I put up with it for years nonetheless, while my poor husband Tony pitched camp at the far edge of our king-size bed.

Sometimes in the bathtub, one of them would point to my breasts and say, "This is where I used to get my milk."

"Right," I would say.

"Can I drink from your boobie now?" would be the next question.

"Nope," I would answer. "We don't do that any more."

Occasionally this would be followed by the plaintive request, "Can I touch one?"

I considered a minute. "Sure, why not."

Then, in a couple of seconds: "Okay, that's enough. Let me wash your back."

Now those days, too, are over. It's happened in stages. The first was when I realized that even if it was okay to be naked around my kids, it might not be okay around somebody else's. This first occurred to me about three years ago, as I was standing dripping wet and stark naked in the kitchen, talking on the phone. I heard the front door open. Good news: It's the kids. Bad news: They've got two neighbors with them, ages six and eleven. Fortunately, it was a portable phone and I had time to flee.

When I got to the bedroom, my eye fell on the two framed portraits of me hanging on the wall, given to me by a photographer friend who did a series of pictures of people without shirts on, hoping, I think, to make an anti-prurient statement by including all ages and sexes and races as subjects. In one of the two black-and-white photographs, I'm nine months pregnant with Vince, whale-like and dreamy, my arms crossed above my pendulous breasts with their big dark nipples pointing earthward. In the other, taken about two weeks after his birth, I am lying on my back beneath a small Mexican painting of Mary. My stomach is flat, my expression is troubled, and my breasts, engorged with milk, are the size of cantaloupes and almost as spherical. They look as if they're about to explode.

The reason I hung these pictures in the bedroom is so the UPS guy won't see them, and I try to remember to take them down when my in-laws are in town. That day, having narrowly escaped greeting Daniel and Joey in the nude, I realized that the boys and their friends might not get the anti-prurient thing either. But I haven't taken the pictures down yet. I'm waiting till the very last minute, which will be the first time I catch them in there on a little field trip with their buddies to ogle Hayes and Vince's mother's tits.

I walk the line, I know it, and am a total libertine compared to many parents. My sons have friends who won't change in front of other boys; I bet those kids' parents are never seen less than clothed. But I don't want us to be like that. I want my kids to know I'm not ashamed of my body and no one else should be, either. The idea that nakedness is something secret and embarrassing is one I just don't buy, and I won't sell to them.

But then there was the night when Hayes was about six and I was getting dressed for an evening out. He was in the bedroom with me, supervising. I held up dresses from the closet and let him choose; he watched me blow-dry my hair and do my makeup. Then, just as I was slipping on my pantyhose, he popped the question. "Can I touch your vagina?"

Well, durn, Hayes, as they say down in Texas, I don't think so. In fact,

I'm quite sure not. As innocent as the suggestion might have been on his part, the questions in my own mind would have tainted it. It had the feel of an experience he would remember, and brood about, and come to feel strange about later on. I, for one, felt strange right then and there.

It was at this same age, six or seven, that I noticed Hayes and his friends starting to work out their interest in the human body among themselves. Girls were chasing the boys, and boys chasing the girls, on the playground; there was loose talk of crushes and who loved whom. In private moments, the ick! facade was dropped altogether, and I witnessed a few sweet instances of tenderness and exploration. For example, we were flying up to my childhood home in New Jersey to visit Nana, and Hayes noticed an adorable little girl in the row behind us. I wish I could have recorded what followed with a hidden camera: the opening scenes of The Opposite Sex, part 2.

Within minutes, he had coerced the cutie pie into the seat beside him; I had been dismissed to sit beside her grandpa. My son was strutting his stuff—writing out the names of his family members and pets, then hers; describing in detail the many wonders of first grade. Most intriguing was their physical interaction: I saw him pat her shoulder, later caress her face, finally touch one of her teeth and ask if she knew its name. An incisor, he told her. What a pick-up line. The six-year-old version of "You have such beautiful lips." A few minutes later, they were actually playing a game in which one of them dropped a crumpled napkin down the back of the other's shirt, then reached in to get it as it fell out the bottom. Jesus, I thought. I hope the grandfather doesn't notice.

But I sure did. I noticed that Hayes was looking at girls. And once he started looking at girls, the rules changed for the somewhat overdeveloped girl he shares a bathroom with. I have had to learn the virtues of a strategically draped towel, perhaps a bathrobe, even a ladylike nightgown. I'm still not as careful as I should be, but at this point even I have started to feel a little uncomfortable on the rare occasions when they catch a flash of maternal nudity and they flat-out stare.

Hayes continues to have great taste in women. Yesterday he invited an adorable and very bright little girl from his third grade class over after school, and he took her to 7-11 on the way home and bought her a Slurpee with his own money. When they got home, he sat her down on the couch and showed her his photo albums. His trip to Disney World. His summer vacation. Him and his dad.

Both of my sons are so cute. It continues to slay me. It continues to make me catch my breath as if I'm noticing for the first time. And—most important from an evolutionary perspective—it continues to make me keep loving them when I forget almost every other reason. Yes, it's different now. A bit more platonic, I suppose. And though I will always miss the easy physical intimacy we shared as mother and baby, I can see that our new kind of closeness, with its preliminary, awkward acknowledgement of the fact that we are opposite sexes, will be no less hard to surrender when the inexorable process of growing up changes everything again.

SHAPESHIFTER

Making the Cut

JAMIE
PEARSON

My second pregnancy had an unanticipated polarizing effect on my husband and me. Things that had seemed insignificant the first time around, like religion, spanking, and preventive dentistry, suddenly became matters of passionate debate. And although we didn't know the sex of our baby—and didn't intend to find out—we lost no time drawing up battle lines about circumcision.

From the first instance of intrauterine cell division until the day our baby was born, we quarreled about circumcision daily. I thought the procedure was cosmetic and barbaric. My husband. Rich, himself a product of a very pro-circumcision family, was undecided.

Very few of our parenting peers had sons. Very few of those who did had opted out of the controversial procedure. Even our best and most liberal friends, Nick and Anna, who slept in a family bed and breastfed until the kids were talking in complex sentences, had circumcised their son Jacob.

"There was only one uncircumcised guy in my entire high school,"

Anna tried to explain over dinner at their house one night. "And everyone knew."

Rich nodded, wide-eyed. Since he was a former jock, locker-room cruelty resonated for him. "Same here," he said. "We called him Slug Dick."

"We had one at our school too," said Nick between bites. "He was called Turtleneck."

The corners of Rich's mouth turned up as he tried not to snicker out of respect for me.

"And there was *another* uncircumcised guy in my fraternity we called Anteater," continued Nick, warming to the topic.

"What, to his face?" I demanded. Beside me Rich laughed beer out his nose. "In front of his parents?"

"Anteater?" said Anna. "I don't get it."

Oblivious to my disapproving vibe, Nick demonstrated with his limp index finger while Rich wheezed and wiped tears from his eyes.

"This just in!" I said, pantomiming newspaper headlines. "Entire world does not revolve around penises."

But mine did.

I read about penises in parenting books, studied penis pictures in my Masters and Johnson sex book, and quizzed neutral friends in private about penises.

Later that week, I met my perennially single college friend, Will, for lunch at a neighborhood bistro. Due to a baby-sitting snafu, I had to bring my eighteen-month-old daughter, Avery, along with her requisite ten pounds of toys. Distractions notwithstanding, it took me only fifteen minutes to settle Avery with a Touch and Feel Farm book, order lunch, and turn the conversation to my preferred topic.

"Well, uncircumcised guys get fewer blowjobs," Will divulged without bothering to lower his voice as we were finishing our salads.

"How exactly do you know that?" I said with a furtive glance over my shoulder. In more than ten years of friendship, I had never had occasion to see Will's penis. "Are you . . . intact?"

"No!" he almost shouted, as if I had questioned his sexual orientation. "No, of course I'm not. It's just common knowledge."

Avery dropped her book. I handed her a stuffed caterpillar. "Says who?" It sounded like more locker-room nonsense to me.

"Well, have you ever done it?" he asked.

Just then our waiter materialized, and I was forced to endure Will's smirk while our entrées were served and Parmesaned.

"No, I haven't," I whispered when the man finally left us. "But not because of *aesthetics*." Avery chucked the caterpillar, so I plied her with a talking Buzz Lightyear. "The opportunity just never arose."

"What about that German guy in college?" Will said, spearing a forkful of *conchiglie* gorgonzola. "Ludwig."

"Stefan," I corrected, coloring at the recollection of that particular rum-fueled summer fling. To my embarrassment, I had no clear memory of Stefan's penis. "The thing is, they all look pretty much the same in the dark," I said.

Will smiled. "So what are you worried about?"

"To infinity and beyond!" opined Buzz as Avery threw him overboard as well.

Which was crueler, I wondered as we moved on to other topics: cutting off the end of a person's penis at birth or thoughtlessly condemning him to a life without fellatio because you were too chicken to do so?

The next weekend, I went to a baby shower for my friend Eva where I brought up Will's blowjob allegation to the group over quiche and fruit salad. Everyone had opinions, but out of the fifteen women present, only Eva's candid colleague Caroline was qualified to speak on the subject.

"It's not all that much different," she said. "And for intercourse, it's actually much better."

"Um, better how?" I finally managed to ask this complete stranger, when it became obvious that no one else was going to.

Although she didn't know anyone at the shower apart from the guest of honor, Caroline gamely picked up a baguette from her plate and demonstrated. "Okay, pretend this is a penis," she said, wrapping her hand over the end of the bread. "Now imagine my hand is the foreskin." She moved the baguette in and out of her cupped palm. "The foreskin stays in place, and creates a protective buffer."

"Ahhhhhhhh," I said. "I see."

"It decreases vaginal friction without decreasing the thrusting sensation," she elaborated with almost clinical detachment. "The woman can have sex every day, and not be sore at all."

I all but skipped home.

I'd always felt more or less confident that Rich would come around to my point of view eventually, but now I knew exactly how to convince him. I'd simply portray uncut penises as mainstream, play up the frequent sex angle, and suppress the unconfirmed blowjob allegation.

I joined Rich and Avery in the living room, where they were playing animal charades. "Hi guys!" I said, kissing them each on the head. "Honey, guess what?"

"Meow," said Rich, snaking across the floor on all fours. He rubbed up against Avery's legs. "What?"

"I met a woman who used to have an uncircumcised boyfriend."

"Cat!" shrieked Avery.

"Right!" said Rich. And then to me, "Please tell me you didn't talk about penises at the baby shower."

I let this pass. "And guess what? She said that sex with an uncircumcised man feels better because there's no friction."

Rich swung his arms and dragged his knuckles on the floor. "Hoo hoo hoo," he said, loping across the floor to where Avery sat nearly exploding with excitement. And then to me, "Isn't friction the whole point?"

"Monkey!"

"Yes!"

I triumphantly brought him up to speed on the foreskin-as-protective-buffer situation, and did the hand thing to illustrate. "The partner of an intact man can have sex *every day* with no discomfort," I told him.

"Neigh," said Rich, galloping in a tight circle around the coffee table. "Neigh, neigh!"

I frowned. This new intelligence wasn't making the impression I had hoped.

At Avery's puzzled look, Rich whinnied and tossed his head in an equine manner.

"Ass?" I suggested.

Rich lobbed a couch pillow at me with Jedi accuracy.

"Horse!" screamed Avery with sudden delight, leaping on Rich's back. "Horse!"

"Right!"

I spent hours that night researching the topic on the Internet in order to better spin the statistics in my favor. "Uncircumcised penises are more sensitive," I said to Rich when I finally came to our room very late. "It's common knowledge."

"That's really hard for me to imagine," replied Rich without looking up from his book. "And I'm honestly not sure it would be a good idea."

I slid into bed beside him and changed tack. "Half of all male infants born in the Western region of the United States were uncircumcised last year," I quoted, tracing the contours of my belly with my fingertips. This was technically true, but only if you included the huge number of babies born to Asian and Central American immigrants.

"Can we take a break from this debate for the rest of the weekend please?" said Rich, turning a page.

I huffily turned off my light.

The next day, while Avery was napping, I went back to the computer. This time I stumbled across a series of horribly explicit photos. In the pictures, a naked newborn boy was shown strapped to a white, plastic board. In the next shot, some kind of metal device was clamped to the end of his penis. In the last picture, a disembodied hand and scalpel had snaked into the frame. It wasn't clear to my uneducated eye whether the tiny foreskin was intact or not, but the baby was screaming.

I was shaken. How had a so obviously Old Testament procedure endured into the twenty-first century? Looking at the last picture again, I tasted bile. Even though I still didn't know the sex of the baby, I vowed I would never allow my hypothetical son to be strapped to that cold, white board. I would never allow anyone to cut off a piece of his body.

I printed the pictures and ambushed Rich in the kitchen.

"You are violating the terms of our ceasefire," he warned when he saw me coming.

"It's genital mutilation," I said.

"We agreed not to talk about this for now."

"You agreed," I said. "Just *look* at this!"

"No."

I dropped the pictures on the counter beside me. "If you can't even look, how can you consider doing this to an innocent child?"

Rich's eyes narrowed. "What about the argument that a son should look like his father?"

"That is *such* bullshit!" I said through clenched teeth. "His penis will be half an inch long and hairless! He won't look like you no matter what we decide!"

Rich bristled. "Can't I have my own opinion?"

"Yes!" I was seething now. "But that's not *your* opinion, it's your mother's!"

Rich rushed to retort, but I didn't let him.

"We can continue this conversation if you like, but the debate is purely academic," I said icily. "If you try to cut off a piece of my baby, I'll leave you."

Rich inhaled sharply. "Really nice," he said, and turned and walked out of the room.

I ran after him and grabbed his arm. "I'm sorry. I didn't mean it."

He turned. "I think you did," he said, staring at me like I was something repulsive he had stepped in. "Why does everything always have to be your way?"

"It doesn't," I replied miserably. "Not always."

"Oh no?"

"No," I said. I put my arms around him, but his hung limply at his sides. He wouldn't look at me and just stared off into the middle distance.

"Just this time," I whispered.

Our baby was born not too many months later.

"It's a boy!" shouted Rich from his post near the sock-covered stirrups that held my feet. Then he squeezed my hand hard. "It's a boy!"

Knowing that jubilant fathers sometimes mistook ropy umbilical cords for tiny penises, I looked to my obstetrician for a second opinion. She smiled and nodded.

It was a boy. We named him Max.

Although the circumcision debate continued right up to the final days of my pregnancy, Rich eventually conceded. I'd like to think I swayed him with my impeccable logic, but really I just wore him down. Many of our friends seemed uncomfortable with our decision and jumped to justify their own choices. They cited the familiar bugaboos of hygiene, teasing, and paternal penis parity. These things still didn't resonate for me, but I didn't pass judgment on my friends either. We had all done what we'd done to protect our sons from pain—that much we had in common.

At three, Max remains blissfully unaware of the controversy surrounding his genital configuration. He is delighted with his foreskin, and joyfully stretches it away from his body, rubber band style, so that he can more easily admire his penis over his protuberant belly on a regular basis. He is happiest naked. While I would never dream of dampening his enthusiasm for self-exploration, I do occasionally find it necessary to set limits. No diddling at the dinner table, for instance.

Although I believe we did the right thing, I still dread the trials to come. Every passing day brings Max closer to locker rooms, summer camps, and slumber parties. I try not to obsess over it, but it's not easy.

"Look at this body," I recently said to Max, while toweling him off after a bath. I pulled him in for a quick, wet hug. "You have a strong, gorgeous, wonderful, delicious, perfect, beautiful body.

He beamed, straightened up, and unconsciously reached for his penis. "I know," he said.

And he does.

(Almost) All Grown Up

MAURA
RHODES

"**O**w! Cut it out!" My fourteen-year-old son dramatically grabs his cheek where I've just plucked out an errant facial hair. These funny little curls are sprouting erratically on Will's otherwise still-baby face, in little clumps, like weeds on a perfectly manicured lawn. On one hand, it's driving me nuts: The random whiskers look really weird. On the other hand, it doesn't seem like there's enough hair on his face to shave, even when you factor in the peach fuzz on his upper lip. It's unmistakably a mustache, but it's so downy and delicate looking, scraping a razor over it seems like a violent act.

There's no question my firstborn son is becoming a man. Besides the facial hair, his voice has deepened, he's long surpassed me in height (I had to reach up to get a grip on that wayward whisker), and his calves are as furry as my husband's. It's like watching a science experiment unfold—one change after another taking place before my very eyes, independent of my input, out of my control.

I seem to be struggling with that last part: I can't quite keep my hands off my evolving boy. Up until now, he was, mostly, in my control. When his nails needed trimming, I clipped them; when he wanted a snack, I made him something healthy; when he outgrew his clothes, I brought home bigger ones and he wore them. Now he does his own clipping (after I nag him about it). When he gets hungry between meals, he gets out a pot and boils water for ramen noodles (typical teen fare, I've discovered) or zaps the frozen taquitas I've succumbed to buying. These mini meals tend to take place within an hour of dinner—a testament to the fact that teenage boys' bellies are never really full.

As for his wardrobe: Will has yet to reach the stage where he cares about looking stylish, but he has very limited and specific ideas about what he'll wear. For example, I can go months without seeing his bare legs because he keeps them covered, even in summer—so those fuzzy legs were quite a shock. He refuses to wear jeans or khakis—preferring pants with an elastic or drawstring waist. (Is he so pressed for time that he can't spare ten seconds for a button and zipper?) Just this morning—we're talking early February in the Northeast—he left the house for a fencing meet with nothing more on his back than a hooded sweatshirt.

I said nothing. I'm learning, very slowly, which battles to wage and which to avoid. Fencing's an indoor sport, I reasoned, so he was probably better off without a jacket and gloves to possibly lose at some high school miles away from home. But I'm not always able to be so sanguine. That's why I find myself plucking hairs off Will's face. I'm like a sculptor on a deadline, constantly shaping and molding my latest masterpiece before it's presented to the world as a finished product: I can't leave him alone any more than he can keep his hands off the single pimple that recently popped up on his chin—something else I keep bugging him about. In fact, to Will, I'm sure I must seem like one of those monkeys that's forever grooming other monkeys, combing through their fur and pinching fleas out of it.

Believe it or not, despite all my figurative nitpicking, I'm loving this stage of my oldest's childhood. I never expected to find male adolescence so fascinating or entertaining. Although I have a brother who's two and a half years younger than I am, when he was Will's age I was nearly seventeen, and the only boys I paid any attention to at the time were the ones I was dating (or wanted to date). I don't think I really had any expectations of life with a teenage boy at all—beyond visions of dirty socks and funny smells. (Will did go through a stinky phase, but now that he's discovered the eye-opening power of the morning shower and has made friends with his antiperspirant, we don't have that problem anymore.) In fact, if anything, I probably dreaded getting to this phase, for a number of reasons:

1. If my son is a teenager, that makes me the mother of a teenager—or rather, a person who's old enough to have a teenage child. I have to admit, Will's thirteenth birthday was as much about me and my vanity as it was about him!

2. Adolescence is just one step away from adulthood—meaning one step away from the ultimate separation, when a child goes off to college or a job.

3. Surely, it would be boring. How could any stage of a child's life be as exciting as the rapid-fire metamorphosis of newborn to toddler, marked by those monumental milestones—first smile, first step, first word? Or the transition to preschool, the first day of kindergarten, or even the fraught middle-school years?

For any new parent reading this, I'm here to say that number three in particular is bunk: As cute as babies are, as entertaining as toddlers are, as amusing as preschoolers and six-year-olds and even ten-year-olds can be, teenagers can be just as cute, entertaining, and amusing. Consider this recent exchange between Will and his dad, my ex-husband, with whom Will spends roughly every other weekend:

JOHN: So, Will, do you have a girlfriend now?

WILL (*in all seriousness*): Yeah—but she's dating someone else.

To me, that innocent little statement is as endearing as anything that came out of Will's mouth when he was little. I thought nothing could top his extrasyllabic mispronunciation of words like "kitten," "mitten," and "button" (kit-e-nen, mit-e-nen, but-e-non); or his response, at age five, when I told him that his father, an actor, would be in a play called *The King and I*, further explaining that the king would be played by someone named Lou Diamond Phillips. "Then is my dad going to be the eye?" Will asked.

I feel the same surge of love and pride when I see Will sitting at the breakfast table reading the *New York Times* or flipping through the *New Yorker* (for the cartoons mostly, I'm sure, but still) as I did when he read his first Dr. Seuss from start to finish. I enjoy our conversations about current events—he has opinions and ideas about the world he's poised to enter in just a few years that can be incredibly enlightening. He asks what I think about touchy subjects, like the war in Iraq and abortion rights—and I find myself constantly amazed that he's even aware of these things—although I suppose that's not giving his social studies teacher a whole lot of credit. And while his taste runs toward movies that are heavy on the martial arts or raunchy comedy, I've managed to drag him to a few films that I wanted to see, using the promise of a supersize Slurpee as bait, and have felt almost as giddy as a schoolgirl with my son at my side. He questions the existence of God, loves sushi, is taking a course in Japanese through our local adult school program, and is writing fan fiction and posting it on the Web. In short, Will has become his own almost man.

Would I feel the same if Will were a girl? I doubt it. For one thing, the physical changes an adolescent female goes through wouldn't be mysterious to me. And I'm already bracing myself for the eye-rolling, sass-saturated, dismissive attitude that I'm certain my now six-year-old daughter is bound to dole out in just a few years: I did it myself to my mom, and I can already see hints of it when Eliza responds to me with a shrug and "Duh." (We're nipping that kind of behavior in the bud for now.)

Which isn't to say that Will's adolescence hasn't come without its share of sarcasm and moaning and complaints. He has his moments. In fact, he sometimes has his hours—hours spent holed up in his room on the third floor of our house playing video games, for example. And he's not above muttering "Jesus" under his breath when I tell him to do something for the umpteenth time, like leave his door at least partially open so that I don't have to stand at the foot of the stairs and yell for ten minutes to call him to the phone or the dinner table. He's not always nice to his younger siblings either, which bothers me to no end, but it's probably unfair of me to expect Will, at fourteen, to be as enamored and as patient with Eliza, and three-year-old Lucas and newborn Wyatt as I am.

But as Will himself would be quick to point out, he's a teenager. His behavior is as appropriate for a kid his age as Lukey's is for a preschooler. I'd be worried if Will weren't easily annoyed by his sister or didn't want to spend time alone in his room. That might make him a little freaky, in fact. I'd rather see him display the irritating kinds of behaviors I remember from my own teenage years than have him act suspiciously nice all the time. I think then I'd have to suspect him of hiding something more than the hair on his legs.

As for the hair on his face, well, that's yet to be addressed. My husband has remarked that it's beginning to look pretty unattractive, but he's reluctant, as Will's stepfather, to step in and hand Will a razor—since Will does, after all, have a very involved biological dad. But my ex hasn't been very proactive on the shaving front either, even though we've talked about it. I'm not sure why that is, but I do know this: It looks like I might be the one who winds up helping my son reach this huge milestone of manhood. And that's okay: I am, after all, still more than willing to keep on molding and shaping and finessing one of my finest works of art: my firstborn, my teenager, my son.

The Teenage Boy

KATIE ALLISON
GRANJU

My eldest child is officially an adolescent. He has put away his action figures and his Legos. He now loves his electric guitar, the band Green Day, and his vintage Ramones t-shirt. He and his middle-school friends are starting a band, they say, but thus far, no one can play their instruments very well. Still, he perseveres, diligently plucking out the same chords from Nirvana songs again and again in his bedroom until he's almost got it right. He reminds me that Sid Vicious and Courtney Love couldn't play their guitars when they were first in bands either.

"Do you know who those people are, Mom?" he asks, eager to explain if I were to tell him that I didn't. Sometimes I do encourage him to tell me things I already know because I enjoy his explanations so much.

He suddenly worries about the way he looks more than he did even six months ago, and he takes a loooooong time to get ready for school in the morning. I can't quite figure this one out, since he wears a uniform, but he insists that it takes time to rumple his khakis and blue oxford button-down into the perfect state of insouciance without crossing a line that will cause the dean of students to admonish him to "use an iron next time."

He has a glorious head of thick, lustrous brown hair—the best in our familial gene pool, as I've been telling him for years—and he has let it grow to the very limit of scholastic permissibility. It's collar-grazingly long and perfectly wavy, and it looks like former teen idol Robby Benson's hair on his best day, circa 1977. It's so beautiful that I sometimes give it an involuntary run-through with my fingers, the way I couldn't stop myself from kissing the top of his head over and over when he was a baby. Now, though, he grimaces when I do this, and then heads back into the bathroom to shake it back into his preferred state of studied disarray.

Unlike all the friends and acquaintances who have warned me that adolescence is the worst part of parenting, I've looked forward to this. My son is interesting and self-sufficient and very, very funny, and I like hearing his take on politics and world events. His talents and deepest passions are blossoming, and he surprises me on a regular basis with things he knows or wants to know. Raising a child is a bit like painstakingly unearthing a precious object over many years. As you carefully chip and brush away, the object slowly reveals its nuances and contours—some of it comfortingly familiar, but much of it a completely unexpected surprise. The surprises have come more frequently lately.

Along with the delightful parts of early adolescence come its horrors. I remember all too well the acute, existential pain of being thirteen years old. Often, lately, when I see my son's clear angst at the end of a long, tiring day of navigating the social minefields of junior high, or as he hangs up after a long, mumbled conversation with someone who sounded female when I answered the phone, I long to do something . . . *anything* to make him feel better.

"She'll call you back," I want to tell him. "Really, and someday you won't even remember her name."

But when I do say things like this, he doesn't believe me, and mostly he doesn't even hear me. It was so much easier when I could gather him up in my arms and rock him and sing to him, and then see him palpably relax and melt into a needed nap as a result of my efforts. We both knew that when he woke up, he would feel all better. The sense of omniscient power that comes with mothering babies and young children was heady for me. I loved having the ability to make the world of someone I loved safe, warm, and intellectually stimulating. Back then, all it took was patience, crayons, and plenty of baby-proofing supplies—like electrical outlet covers. It was easy enough to create our own self-contained happy, happy universe, where he knew that all was right with the world and my worries were minimal.

Now his world is becoming increasingly beyond my control. I can't prevent cruel kids from saying what they will say or chronically unhappy teachers and coaches from venting their adult pain onto my son. I know that his heart will be broken, sooner rather than later, by some girl who has no idea what she's doing. I know that far too soon he will see the first of his friends make choices that threaten to ruin their lives and that he too will be faced with these choices.

These are things that I know with a great deal of certainty will happen to my son, and for the most part, they are completely beyond my ability to prevent. But I'll continue to try. I hope that the years we spent together in the warm cocoon of his early childhood offered him some immunization against the slings and arrows of adolescence. I hope that the slips of the hand that I've made in unearthing the man he is becoming haven't banged him up or scarred him too terribly.

Mostly, I hope he will continue to talk to me and tell me or show me what I can do—or not do—to support and guide him in finding his own way. Really, I think that's increasingly all that's left for a mother of a teen-age boy to do.

The Day He Was Taller

JACQUELYN
MITCHARD

We all tend to use the big words like small change: "My jaw dropped. . . ." "It took my breath away. . . ."

But rarely do we mean or even understand them.

And then something happens, and sometimes it's something small, that lets us see why those phrases were invented and what they were meant to convey.

I rushed home from a book reading I'd promised to do, a couple of seasons ago, on a Saturday, hoping against faint hope that my teenage son would be waiting, spiffed and scrubbed, for the friend's bar mitzvah service we were expected to attend in half an hour.

I said the hope was faint.

It really was infinitesimal.

A golden certainty told me that Rob would be either (a) at the tail end of a twenty-seven-minute shower or (b) rampaging around his room muttering darkly that he had no clothes.

It was (b).

When I hollered upstairs, Rob said, "I'm ready!"

Now, I've been a mother for a very long time, to a rather large number of sons and daughters. And normally I greet announcements like these with the same credence I give my eight-year-old when she tells me there is a cow in the yard. (There once, however, actually was a cow in the yard. And once a hot-air balloon.)

Rob was dressed.

But he really didn't have any clothes.

He'd outgrown every stitch he owned, including socks, and would have had to attend the bar mitzvah party, just hours away, in pants that would have been more appropriately termed "capris." We hurriedly went to the temple, greeted our friends, and sat unobtrusively through the service.

And then we dashed from the service to a department store.

"Robert," I said, in what I hoped was an empowering way, "you do not respect my opinion in matters of clothing. I do not mind. Go into the men's department and find yourself something you would be happy to wear tonight at a big, fancy party with many of my friends."

We didn't really connect again until dinnertime, when I found myself again pacing downstairs, dressed in minor finery and ready for the bar mitzvah party. And, in truth, it had been a summer when we hadn't connected much. Rob had gone on several trips, including a wilderness adventure. I felt we'd spent three months waving to each other in airports.

Now, he came down the stairs, and my jaw dropped.

He wore a suit with a discreet black-on-black pattern, and a jet stud replaced a tie at the neck of his cranberry-colored dress shirt. Wet-comb marks grooved his longish blond hair. He looked so handsome, I couldn't find words that wouldn't have embarrassed him; so I just kissed him on the cheek.

And that was when I noticed it. To kiss him, I had to stand on my tiptoes.

Robert and I had begun the summer the same size—the size I'll always be, about five feet four inches. This was an experience unprecedented in two decades of motherhood.

I was mother to a bigger person.

In a few sunny strung-together weeks, Rob had grown so tall that, even wearing heels, I had to look up. And in a few hours, between that morning and this night, something in the calculus between us had changed. We both felt it. It was not sad. It was poignant, like watching from the sidelines as an exhausted runner slams into the tape—the feeling that much as you could empathize, much as you could see right in front of you, you still could never know.

I thought of two things.

The first was that stylish jet collar stud. Robert had never owned a tie, not even the clip-on kind you give to baby boys.

I thought of perhaps the saddest thing that Rob's dad, Dan, had ever told me. It was this: Just days before Dan's father died of a heart attack, he had been teaching Dan, his oldest son, to make a Windsor knot. Dan was a young teenager then, about the age Robert was that balmy Saturday evening.

When Rob was not quite ten, long before shaving, long before the tying of ties, Dan died of cancer.

And so, I also thought of the conferring of manhood, which fathers ordinarily do for their sons in various ways. I thought of the part in the old ritual of bar mitzvah, in which a boy takes his full place as a member of the Jewish community of worship. The traditional thing to say is, "Today, you are a man."

We are not Jewish, and there is no ritual for us that is quite the same. I'm also not a father. So I didn't say those words. Not out loud.

But implicitly we both knew, from the gentle silence between us, that they had been spoken. When we got out of the car, Rob didn't take my hand, as once he would have.

I took his arm.

Time has passed, and now all but one of my sons is taller than I. When I stand among the elder ones, I'm a stump in a forest of redwoods and willows.

But none of their growth, though it has always affected me, has had quite the power that the first, most obvious, most wistful moment with Rob had, as we pulled our car up to the hotel where the party would be held.

The sense that life is lived forward but understood backward—as Kierkegaard said—was sharp. We walked out into the warm fall evening together, as the people we had become, a short woman in a long blue dress and a taller, good-looking young man, in a good black suit.

Shapeshifter

MELANIE LYNNE
HAUSER

In the dark recesses of folklore and mythology, there are whispers of shadowy beings known as shapeshifters. These elusive creatures are rumored to take on different physical forms, morphing from animal to man and back again. The two coexist, fighting for control of the physical body; the battle is fascinating, troubling, and often terrifying for the innocent victim who happens upon it.

Shapeshifters walk among us, even now. They dress in t-shirts and jeans in order to blend in; they try not to call attention to themselves because conformity is their greatest goal. They eat typical American food, nothing exotic or distinctive, only giving themselves away by the enormous quantities of this food that they can inhale in one sitting. They speak our language—or at least a version of it, putting far too much emphasis on the phrase "I don't know."

Apparently, in their native tongue, this simple sentence represents a variety of thoughts ranging from "I don't wish to continue this conversation" to "I actually know the grade I received on my trigonometry exam but don't wish to tell you at this time because I know you'll freak out and quite frankly, I'm not in the mood." Our common interpretation of the phrase—"I lack the information necessary to accurately answer your question"—is rarely used.

But you will continue to ask the questions anyway. You must. Because you are a twenty-first-century victim of the curse of the shape-shifter. Or to put it in terms so horrific that I beg of you, please try to stifle your scream:

You are the mother of a teenage boy.

Look at the creature, his hairy toes peeking out of flip-flops even though it's thirty degrees out and snowing. Today he is cool. Too cool for words. He walks five feet ahead of you, his hands in his pockets or held stiffly by his side, his shoulders hunched forward because he is always just a little afraid that everyone in the entire world is looking at him. And just in case they are, he would rather they not figure out that the smiling, nodding woman running after him—actually pausing to converse with people! People she knows!—is his mother. And so he strides ahead, his face a mask of coolness. You could be run down by a rogue Segway, your legs cut off, your embarrassing Mom shoes (sensible snow boots; how lame!) sticking out from under the scooter like ruby slippers, and the beast wouldn't care. He would keep on walking, unable to *believe* how embarrassing it is that you are stuck there on the sidewalk like a chewed-up piece of bubblegum.

Unless, of course, he needed money. Then he might be persuaded to slow down. A little.

Fine, you say, resolving never again to speak to him. Resolving to let him go his own way; you'll meet up whenever, he's a big boy now, an adult, even—look how tall he is! Look at those ropy muscles, those knotty hands, the hairy legs, stubble on his upper lip. The condescending smirk, just like a man's, whenever you dare to voice an opinion. He doesn't need you. He's perfectly capable of taking care of himself; doesn't he tell you that a dozen times a day? Hasn't he actually written it on his bedroom door, which is shut from the moment he gets home from school to the moment he gets up in the morning; you shudder at the unholy thought of what he's *doing* in there. So let him. Let him take care of himself.

But watch out. You don't even see it coming. Because next thing you know:

Shapeshifter.

"Mom," he's wailing, just a few hours later. "Can you make me cookies? My favorites? You know, the ones with sprinkles?" He smiles, he comes up and puts his arms around you—not the other way around; you'll never be able to put your arms around him ever again, because your head comes up to approximately his collarbone. His eyes squeeze shut as he's hugging you and somehow, with those famous eyes at the back of your head, you can see this. Then he whispers. "*Mommy.*"

You both stiffen slightly—did he really say that? You do him the enormous favor of pretending that you didn't hear it. But your heart knows. It skips a beat, because you've just been handed a present—a ghostly glimpse of your special little guy. That little tiger who held your hand so trustingly in public, chattering away, unable to stop himself from telling you every thought as it popped into his head. The child has, just for a moment, wrestled the body from the man. And you smile contentedly, relieved. He still needs you, this son of yours—what were you worried about? Who else is going to make him cookies, bring him water in the middle of the night, tell him the funny story about the time he drew on his baby brother with permanent markers?

So you bustle around, making the cookies; you arrange them on a special plate and pour him a vat of milk and watch while he eats, marveling at how he can fold five cookies into his mouth at a time and wash them down with one gulp, no chewing necessary. He actually thanks you, again with a hug, and you almost ruin it by crying. But you don't. You go to bed happy, your children safe and sound underneath your roof, as they always will be. Until:

Shapeshifter.

The next day he's talking on the phone. Behind closed doors. His voice is suddenly deep and manly, hushed but for the occasional chuckle, and you hear the name "Caitlin." Once again your heart skips a beat, but not in a good way. *Caitlin.* Who is this hussy? You've never met a Caitlin before—unless, could it be? Is she that siren who used to play on his soccer team, the one who always clipped the sleeves of her jersey so that it looked like a tank top? No matter. Because even if you've never met this Caitlin before, you know her type. Oh boy, do you know her type! All firm breasts, narrow hips, and low-slung jeans; glossy long hair, Jezebel eyes. She's clearly offering up something more delectable than a plateful of *cookies*.

Suddenly you see the future more clearly. The future where you're sitting all alone on Christmas morning, waiting for the obligatory phone call because they're at *her* parents' house, once again. You prepare for this inevitability by imagining fancy little Italian motor scooters and long European cruises, telling yourself—and that hairy-toed creature who happens to live under your roof, devouring all your food—that you're looking forward to the day when he moves out and goes to college. What a relief it will be! What a load off! No more smelly tennis shoes, no more yellow rings around the toilet. Let someone else—Caitlin, perhaps?—burn her fingers while making him cookies with *sprinkles*.

You tell yourself this, but you don't believe it. Neither does he. Because you—are not a shapeshifter.

You are, and will always be, a mother. *His* mother.

Oh, you try to fool yourself. You try to treat him like the adult he insists he is. You sit down next to him one night—right next to him, on the couch, oh the horror!—and confide in him some of your most grown-up thoughts. Sometimes you're concerned about money, you say, shaking your head. For instance, what if you can't save enough for retirement and you end up in a state-run nursing home eating watery pudding and watching *The Price Is Right* until you fall into a coma? What does he think about that?

He squirms, scratches his armpits, looks away, and quietly informs you that he really didn't need to know any of this. Then he holds out his huge mitt of a hand and asks for his allowance.

How unfair! *He* may be able to morph into that little puppy with the cowlick one minute, the hairy man the next; taking one last lingering look at childhood, yet eager for the future. Demanding cookies while making dates. But not you. You must always remain the Mom. A fancy little Italian motor scooter? Ha! You'll still be driving a minivan when you're seventy and you know it. So does he. He's counting on it, actually. And maybe, in a way, you're counting on him counting on it, hoping that he'll come back and visit you, that you'll get another cherished glimpse of that little boy you miss, the one you'll remember for the rest of your life, long after the man has won the battle and claimed the body for good.

Because that's what mothers do: We wait. After our bodies have morphed through the rigors of childbearing, we become frozen, tethered in place by stretch marks and apron strings. We keep watch. And we become the caretakers, passing down from generation to generation the tale of the mythological creature, half man, half child. All ours.

"Do you remember?" you will ask. At every Christmas, every Thanksgiving, every family celebration for years to come.

"I don't know," he'll say with a shrug. "How about those cookies?"

So you will smile to yourself, make the cookies (Caitlin never could get them right, what an idiot she turned out to be, after all), because you do remember. You'll always remember. You get the memories of both—the child and the man.

While the shapeshifter only knows the memory of you. Mom.

Mommy, on certain occasions, which you both have the decency never to mention.

Space Invader

LISA
PEET

Space Invaders, the video game, came out in 1978. I remember that because it was the last year I actually thought going to the mall might be interesting. Or rather, it was when I gave up on that particular aspect of trying to be like every other girl in the ninth grade.

As a way to blend in, going to the mall should have been easy—all I had to do was get someone to drive me over on a Saturday afternoon. Assimilation didn't get much simpler than that. But as part of my grand get-normal project, mall-going wasn't an unqualified success. I went about it all wrong. When I got there, I'd head straight for the comic book store, then the record store, finally ending up at Spencer Gifts to snicker at the edible underwear and the dirty Mad Libs books. What I was supposed to be doing, of course, was hanging out with everyone else at the pizza place and Baskin-Robbins and the arcade. What I was supposed to be doing in that mall in 1978 was looking at boys.

In retrospect, I don't think I was quite that unwitting. Honestly, I probably knew exactly what was expected of me as a red-blooded American teenage girl. Deep down, overshadowed by my innate dorkiness, was a grasp of my basic problem: I thought teenage boys were awful. And nothing, *nothing*, was more awful than a teenage boy playing *Space Invaders*.

Those were the days when arcades were still mostly all pinball machines, with a scattering of air hockey, Skee-Ball, and the claw that never caught a single decent prize. Now, pinball, that involved some kind of physical interaction, and someone playing pinball was fairly engaged. A boy deep into his second round of bonus points was a bundle of nerves and insistent hair-trigger movements, an expression on his face of agonized expectation that we would all learn to identify a few years later as the tip-off that he was about to come.

But those were also the heady, post–*Star Wars* days of nascent video games. There was *Pong*, which was for losers; *Breakout*, which was for your little brother; and then there was *Space Invaders*, which every boy between the ages of twelve and seventeen was hopelessly hot for. They lined up three and four deep to play, shirts untucked, elbowing each other in the ribs and throwing random glances at the girls, then going back to shuffling their enormous, sneakered feet. And when each one finally found himself in front of the machine, he would feed in his quarters and instantly go slack-jawed. None of the feral grunting that accompanied pinball; *Space Invaders* boys were eerily quiet. Sometimes their faces twitched violently, mirroring their fingers, but otherwise they wore scary, hollow expressions that could only be described as slightly retarded.

Add to the blank faces zits. Add lanky longish hair and blooming BO. Add inexpertly shaved facial growth that looked a lot like dirt, or alternately those embarrassing pink peach-fuzzy cheeks. *Dawn of the Dead* came out in 1978 too, that movie in which a horde of zombies rises up and overruns a deserted shopping mall. I don't believe that was a coincidence.

As far as I was concerned, not only had empty-eyed zombies taken over the mall, but I was supposed to find them attractive and hopefully get one to take me to the movies and put his hand up my shirt.

I just never liked teenage boys. Not ever. When I was little, my friends' older brothers were weird and loud and didn't appeal to me in the least. Once everyone hit puberty and started hooking up with one another in age-appropriate fashion, I developed fierce, silent crushes on my father's graduate students. When I lost my virginity in high school, it was to a friend's college-age brother; she held this against me, for some reason, for years. What was to like about them? They were smelly and sweaty, all forebrain and no finesse. As soon as I was out of high school, I breathed a sigh of relief: I was off the hook. I'd never have to look at another teenage boy again.

Well, not exactly.

True, I would never again be expected to choose from an available pool of partners who were too young to drink or vote. I would date men who were far too old for me, and then as the years went by, the gap would shrink. I would marry someone seven years my senior. I would have a baby, get divorced, end up living with a guy who was nearly my age, and split up with him too. As I got older, the men, as it were, got younger.

And eventually I ended up living with a teenage boy.

Not on purpose. It wasn't like I rethought my options and realized that I had been wrong all those years, that I could regain my youth by robbing the cradle, that fresh meat was the sweetest. No, it was that my baby, that sweet-smelling, wide-eyed, adoring little creature who nursed and toddled and ate his vegetables, somehow, all of a sudden, turned into a six-foot-tall big-footed brute himself.

There's a line all parents use at one point or another when their children are small and have done something annoying or messy or loud. "It's a good thing he's so cute," you say, shaking your head ruefully. "That's how they survive. Otherwise you'd just want to kill them." It's always funny when you say it. Everyone chuckles knowingly. But in retrospect it's just sad, because before you know it, they're not that cute and you still can't kill them. Those days of unalloyed sweetness are fairly numbered. There's another line that every parent hears: "Enjoy them while they're little—it goes by so fast." This is true as well. The years when they're tiny and sweet may look endless stretching out from the vantage point of new parenthood, spit-up, and sleepless nights. But when you view them from the other end of the telescope, you realize what a brief time it actually was. Not only that, but when you find yourself at that point of nostalgia, you're usually still stuck with the giant changeling on your hands for a few more years.

I don't mean to paint a terrible picture of my particular teenage boy. He's not a Satanist or a stoner. He's a pretty decent kid who gets good grades, has a job, and kisses the dog. But I constantly find myself readjusting, reconciling the grinning little boy whose photo is on my refrigerator with the Other. I have my own personal shopping-mall zombie now. His size-12 boots reverberate through the house; his soggy towels turn up behind the bathroom door. The slack-jawed video game warrior who disgusted me twenty-five years ago is a fixture now, installed complacently on my couch playing *Grand Theft Auto*. It's enough to make me nostalgic for *Space Invaders*.

And yet this is my baby. Underneath the hair and funk and general oblivion is the same sweet boy. It's easy to forget he's there, but not so hard to remember, either.

I wonder sometimes if my feelings would be less complicated had I been one of those ninth-grade girls with an actual boyfriend. Because although much of my dislike for teenage boys was on aesthetic grounds, they were also scary, and often mean. All that posturing and flirting was only fun if they liked you back, and I spent those years more concerned with avoiding embarrassment than getting asked out. Teenage boys had been known to roll down their car windows and bark at girls. It had happened to someone I knew, not to me, but I lived in fear of that kind of public humiliation. If one of those *Space Invaders* guys had smiled at me and wanted to walk down the street holding hands, I would have ignored the most horrendous, oozing acne you could imagine. I would have done anything. I would have done *anything*. I can't get back at those boys for not loving me—but then again I can, by loving mine no matter what. It's a funny form of retribution.

So it's true, I don't find teenage boys any more charming now than I did when I was fourteen, and I know I don't do a seamless job of pretending otherwise. On the other hand, I know that my son is absolutely sure of how much I adore him. I may be easily annoyed, I may ask more than my share of rhetorical questions that involve the phrase "Excuse me, are you *blind?*" and I may be sick enough of arguing to throw up my hands and let him play *Grand Theft Auto* as much as his little heart desires. But he knows I love him. He's not going to be the kind of guy who needs to avenge himself on the world. My work here is almost finished; I think I did okay. And I'm reasonably sure he'll never roll down his car window and bark at some poor, furtive girl whose only wish in life is to grow up, get out of high school, and never have to look at another teenage boy again.

Surrounded by Children

KATHRYN BLACK

Important messages sometimes arrive in disguise. But that's not what was on my mind the day a friend called to say that Genevieve, a clairvoyant she'd met years ago, would be passing through town and was taking appointments for readings. I didn't let her question get past "Do you want—" before I jumped in with "Yes!"

In our college days, my girlfriends and I regularly went to tea leaf and palm readers, and once visited a psychic who dissected our relationships, current and past, with creepy accuracy. In adulthood, though, I'd come to regard friends, therapists, meditation, and prayer as more reliable sources of insight. So what made me leap at the chance for a reading? The day I heard of Genevieve's visit, I needed all the help I could get divining my future. I was forty-one and had just found out that I was pregnant for the first time, ever.

Although into my second trimester, I was still walking around in a stunned-thrilled-terrified fog. I'd spent decades successfully avoiding children, only to approach forty and be faced with the wretched question

Where are my babies? Rounding that forty-year mark, my life had taken a radical turn, driven by forces I still don't quite understand, though one of them surely was baby longing. My first marriage—long and childless—ended. I moved fifteen hundred miles, married a man I'd known since childhood, and against the odds and reason, had gotten pregnant. Any bead on my future would be welcome.

That's how I came to be sitting across from a psychic one spring afternoon, awaiting her divinations. I wasn't showing yet, but how could she miss seeing that I was lit up with excitement and trepidation over all that giving birth might mean to me and my life?

Genevieve, however, plunged into dissecting my career, giving me all sorts of welcome encouragement. Suddenly she said, "Do you have children?"

"I'm pregnant."

"Boohoo, your first one. I think of children as the ultimate adventure." I wanted reassurance that my baby would be healthy, that my life wouldn't become unrecognizable, that my marriage would flourish, that I'd live through childbirth. But she didn't want to talk about any such thing. With a wave of her hand, she moved on, saying, "I see you surrounded by children."

I didn't hear much after that. I hadn't even baby-sat since I was a teenager. *How could this one undeveloped miracle in my body turn into something as unimaginable as "surrounded by children"?*

On the way home in the car, my friend and I compared notes on what we'd gleaned, but then I didn't give my adventure with the clairvoyant a thought. Not for a few years, anyway.

That miracle in my body became my husband's and my beloved infant boy. Six months into his life, we visited friends to meet their newborn. As my husband and I walked to our car afterward, we, pretty much simultaneously, had a mind-blowing revelation. We turned to one another, and one of us, I don't remember who, said, "We could do this again." It's hard to believe now, but we had not thought of having a second child. Who is handed a long-awaited, unexpected gift, valuable beyond measure, and says, "Nice. Where's the next one?" Not us, but that day walking away from our friends' mountain home, in sunshine and the scent of pine, we dared think we could have another baby. Fourteen months later, our second boy was born. My husband was forty-two, I was forty-three, big brother was twenty months. Did we wish for a girl? No. Then, as now, gratitude was the governing emotion. Again, we could not look at this second precious gift—*another* perfect, healthy boy—and wish a single cell of his body be different, much less his gender.

We settled into life with our wee boys, and as the years passed, I slowly came to realize that what I'd mistaken for a clairvoyant's toss-away comment was instead the guiding theme of my life. Over the next dozen years, I had many moments when I heard Genevieve's prediction. It never failed to make me smile, and I know now that it resonated deep within me the moment she said it and helped change how I saw myself. It helped me leap across the divide from trying-to-be-sophisticated career woman to woman surrounded by children. And I jumped right over gender issues. I have never identified myself as mother to boys, but as mother to children. And I have lots of children.

I would hear the voice of Genevieve as I stood in my kitchen with my two preschoolers and three or four other munchkins crowded around, waiting, while I whipped up peanut butter crackers and sliced apples for their afternoon snack. Or I'd be herding the lot of them to the park so they could play their favorite made-up games. One day I opened the door to the basement playroom to see it transformed by the neighborhood children into an elaborate construction employing every chair, table, blanket, sheet, towel, and pillow they could get their hands on. They drew me into the dark tunnels, showing me where each pretend baby animal lived. On my hands and knees, I giggled with them. My fate had been sealed that day sitting across from the psychic, and it has been good for me and for all my children.

One of the surprising and delightful benefits of being a mother, for me, has been that most of those children are not my own. My husband and I stopped at a modest two, but those two have brought to me relationships with the offspring of others, mostly our friends and neighbors. And, of course, a good half are girls.

Thanks to other people's children, I've not been entirely deprived of girl stuff, even though I gave birth to boys. First grader Emma and I have done our nails together in the same jazzy tangerine. I have prepared to walk the neighborhood children to school, with just enough time to make it if we all run down the hill, when Rachel shows up in her flip-flops. I have been dubbed "fairy godmother" by my first goddaughter. I have shopped for that girl at Laura Ashley only to select a puff-sleeved, flowered number with billowy pant legs that made her burst into furious tears. Unbeknownst to me, she had decided on a dresses-only policy, which she stuck to for years. I have received a ceramic bunny for Mother's Day from Logan, which now has a permanent place on my shelf of treasures. I have smelled the newborn head of my second goddaughter. Maybe this is part of why I've never stopped to yearn for a daughter of my own. Maybe hearing the psychic's prediction so long ago assured me that, one way or another, girls as well as boys would come to me.

The role these children play in my life goes beyond gender, however. This arrangement of opening my home and self to other people's children—just as they open theirs to mine—benefits us all. None in my tribe are deprived in any way. Not one needs the second home I provide, but children can't have too many caring adults in their lives. The young ones who freely come and go in my house, those I've known all or most of their lives, had some of their first experiences with exploring the world beyond their own nests right here in mine. Those children, who know the rules around the computer in our house, who know where I keep the plastic cups for drinks and which pantry shelf they can snack from, who know I freely dispense Band-Aids and sympathy, are getting their inborn need for human connection met, in part, right here, with my sons, my husband, and me.

Research has long told us that all humans need nurture, first with parents and then with wider communities, in order to grow up healthy, whole, and ready for a productive life. Children do best when parents especially, but also other adults in their world, are both warm and careful to set limits and restrictions.

I know I provide one of those safe, secure, and nurturing places for the handful of children in my sphere of influence. And I'm thankful my boys have other homes where they can comfortably share a meal, spend the night, be held accountable for "thank you" and "please." The surprise has been how rewarding providing those connections for other children has been for me.

One of the rewards has been discovering how enriching and healing motherhood can be. My own boys, by their very nature, in their helpless beginnings, demanded that I find purpose in meeting their needs. And then right before my eyes and under my diligent care, they have grown and flourished.

Parenting is like good therapy. It provides an experience of being in the world and of relating to others in a new way. And, like therapy, it's not necessarily easy or comfortable. Both my children and those I've collected have been teachers and agents of change.

My own came loaded with not only potential and hope, but also the likelihood that they would reveal my most humbling faults. And they have, not once, but again and again. When my younger son was two, he asked to do something, and before I could answer, he hung his head and said, "But we don't have time." Maybe the struggle to change how I view time in my own head (*I'm late, I'm late*) hasn't budged, but I've tried hard to stop conveying that to my boys. My mothering has helped them grow, but it has also pushed me to mature and change, as well.

My sons have helped me to see what's important, on many levels. They've encouraged me to slow down, get to church, and eat more organic food. Most important, they shoved work out of the center of my life and put themselves and my husband and the family we've created right in the middle. They've taught me that I'm brave beyond measure because I allow myself to love them fully, knowing our time together is limited.

Often, however, I find it easiest to be my best mother self around other children. With my own, I'm sorry to say, I'm capable of lapsing into old habits—lashing out with sarcasm or silent rejection—but when I'm in charge of others, I'm more likely to rise to a higher level. One day, when my younger boy was six, one of his favorite playmates, Eli, visited for a long afternoon. Over the hours, their rambunctiousness wore me down, and when I said it was time to clean up and get ready to end the playtime, they ignored me. My patience was frayed, but as I approached my son's bedroom, I found I wasn't angry, just tired. I didn't want to bully my own child, and certainly not sweet Eli, whose mother had entrusted his care to me. I sat down and gave them a short, good speech about how they had not chosen to do the right thing, so now I would watch until they had cleaned up the mess. I was kind and firm, direct and effective, just as I want to be every time.

Some days later, Eli's mother told me that he said, "Kathryn never yells or gets mad." Not true, of course, but what he didn't know was that his presence in our home helped me reach for a better way to be.

When our second son was newly born, our young family went to a picnic in a friend's backyard. A man, father to several and grandfather to many, asked me whether my husband and I were going to try for a daughter next. I laughed and said, "No, we have two healthy, beautiful children. I've pressed my luck as an elderly primipara as far as I want to."

"That's good," he replied. "There's no sense filling up the backyard with boys waiting for a girl."

It turned out that our backyard—and basement and family room and kitchen—has been plenty full of boys and girls without my giving birth to every one of them. And I'm blessed by them all. Surrounded by children, I've found, means surrounded by love.

Notes

From the Introduction

Transcript of Harvard president Larry Summers's remarks (January 14, 2005) available at www.president.harvard.edu/speeches/2005/nber.html.

Agnès Lacreuse, Charles B. Kim, Douglas L. Rosene, Ronald J. Killiany, Mark B. Moss, Tara L. Moore, Lakshmi Chennareddi, and James G. Herndon, "Sex, Age, and Training Modulate Spatial Memory in the Rhesus Monkey (Macaca Mulatta)," *Behavioral Neuroscience* 119, no. 1. (February 2005). Full text of the article is available from the American Psychological Association Public Affairs Office and at www.apa.org/journals/releases/bne1191118.pdf.

Julianna Kettlewell, "Female Chromosome Has X Factor: Females Are Genetically More Varied Than Males, an Analysis of the X Chromosome Has Revealed," *BBC News*, March 16, 2005, http://news.bbc.co.uk/2/hi/science/nature/4355355.stm.

"The Human Genome: X Chromosome"
www.nature.com/nature/focus/humangenome/x.html
www.sanger.ac.uk/HGP/ChrX/

Rick Weiss, "Human X Chromosome Coded: Sequence Confirms How Sex Evolved and Explains Some Male-Female Differences," *Washington Post*, March 17, 2005, p. A03, available at www.washingtonpost.com/wp-dyn/articles/A41919-2005Mar16.html.

Contributors

STEPHANY AULENBACK'S work has appeared in a number of magazines and literary journals, including *McSweeney's*, and she is a frequent contributor to the literary weblog MaudNewton.com. One of her short stories was recently nominated for a Pushcart Prize.

KAREN E. BENDER is the author of a novel, *Like Normal People*. Her fiction has appeared in the *New Yorker*, *Granta*, *Zoetrope*, *Ploughshares*, *Story*, and other magazines, and it has appeared in the *Best American Short Stories* and *Pushcart Prize* anthologies. She has received grants from the Rona Jaffe Foundation and the National Endowment for the Arts. She teaches fiction writing in the creative writing program at the University of North Carolina at Wilmington, where she lives with her husband, novelist Robert Anthony Siegel, and their two children.

KATHRYN BLACK, author, essayist, and lecturer, conducts workshops based on her most recent book, *Mothering Without a Map: The Search for the Good Mother Within*. Black is also author of the award-winning book *In the Shadow of Polio: A Personal and Social History*, which was named by the *Boston Globe* one of the best nonfiction books of 1996. Recipient of the

Colorado Book Award for Literary Nonfiction and named 1997 Author of the Year by the American Society of Journalists and Authors, Black is a former editor at *Woman's Day* and *Better Homes & Gardens* magazines and has written for numerous other national magazines, including *Child, Psychotherapy Networker, House Beautiful, Yoga Journal,* and *Food & Wine.* She lives in Boulder with her husband and children. For more information, visit her website at www.motheringwithoutamap.com.

ROBIN BRADFORD is an award-winning fiction writer and essayist. Her work has appeared most recently in *Mother Knows: 24 Tales of Motherhood* and *Three-Ring Circus: How Real Couples Balance Marriage, Work, and Family.* Her monthly column, "Motherload," appears at www.austinmama .com. An O. Henry Award winner, Bradford has been a Dobie Paisano Fellow and Texas Literature Grant recipient. Bradford works as a fundraiser for an affordable housing nonprofit in Austin, Texas, where she lives with her husband, son, three cats, and a dog. Her home office was formerly a walk-in closet.

GAYLE BRANDEIS is the author of *Fruitflesh: Seeds of Inspiration for Women Who Write* and *The Book of Dead Birds: A Novel,* which won Barbara Kingsolver's Bellwether Prize for Fiction in Support of a Literature of Social Change. Her other cool Barbara-related honors include a grant from the Money for Women/Barbara Deming Memorial Fund and a Barbara Mandigo Kelly Peace Poetry Award. She was named a 2004 Writer Who Makes a Difference by the *Writer* magazine. She is Writer in Residence for the Mission Inn Foundation's Family Voices project and is on the faculty of the UCLA Writers Program. She lives in Riverside, California, with her husband and two children.

ANDREA J. BUCHANAN is a writer living in Philadelphia. Her book of essays on motherhood, *Mother Shock: Loving Every (Other) Minute of It*, is available wherever books are sold. She is managing editor of Literary-Mama.com, an online literary magazine for the maternally inclined. Her work has been featured in the *Christian Science Monitor*, *Parents* magazine, and *Nick Jr.* magazine; in the collection *Breeder: Real-Life Stories from the New Generation of Mothers*; and in online parenting magazines. In addition to editing the anthologies *It's a Boy* and *It's a Girl*, she is also the coeditor of *Literary Mama: Reading for the Maternally Inclined* and has work forthcoming in *The Imperfect Parent* and *About What Was Lost: 20 Writers on Miscarriage*. You can read more about her adventures in motherland at her website, www.andibuchanan.com.

FAULKNER FOX is the author of *Dispatches from a Not-So-Perfect Life: Or How I Learned to Love the House, the Man, the Child.* Her essays and poems have recently appeared in *Salon*, *Parenting*, *Child*, and *Feminist Studies*. She teaches creative writing at Duke University and lives in Durham, North Carolina, with her husband and their two sons.

KATIE ALLISON GRANJU is the author of *Attachment Parenting: Instinctive Care for Your Baby and Young Child* and a contributor to several anthologies. Her articles and essays have appeared in *Salon*; the *Chicago Tribune*; *Cooking Light*; *Pregnancy*; *Parenting*; *Brain, Child*; *Hip Mama*; and many other publications. She is the single mama of Henry, Jane, and Elliot and lives in the foothills of the Great Smoky Mountains. Her website is www.katieallisongranju.com.

ONA GRITZ is the mother of eight-year-old Ethan. She is the author of two children's books, *Starfish Summer* and *Tangerines and Tea*. Her poetry has appeared or is forthcoming in several anthologies and literary journals, including the *Paterson Literary Review*, *Poetry East*, the *American Voice*, *Literary Mama*, the *Pedestal Magazine*, and *Ekphrasis*, where she was a finalist for the 2004 Ekphrasis Prize.

GWENDOLEN GROSS, dubbed "the reigning queen of women's adventure fiction" by *Book* magazine, is the author of *Field Guide* and *Getting Out*. She's won awards for her writing workshops, and she has published essays, poems, and stories in dozens of journals and anthologies of the more traditional variety, as well as those made with staples, feathers, Post-its, used popsicle sticks, googly eyes, and glitter, and edited by her son and daughter. She lives in northern New Jersey.

MELANIE LYNNE HAUSER lives outside of Chicago with her husband and two teenage boys, who provide her with endless inspiration and occasional frustration. Her first novel, *Confessions of Super Mom*, has just been released, with the sequel to follow in 2006. Her stories have been published in the *Adirondack Review* and *In Posse Review* and have been performed on Chicago's National Public Radio's *Stories on Stage* program.

MARRIT INGMAN is a regular contributor to the *Austin Chronicle*. Her writing has also been printed and syndicated by *Brain, Child*; *Isthmus*; the *Coast Weekly*; AlterNet; *Clamor*; the *Anchorage Press*; *Mamalicious*; and other publications. She has taught at Boston University, Southwestern University, and Springfield College. Her essays are also featured in several anthologies, including *Mamaphonic: Balancing Mothering and Other Creative Acts* and

Secrets and Confidences: The Complicated Truth About Women's Friendships. Her first book, a memoir of postpartum depression entitled *Inconsolable: How I Threw My Mental Health Out with the Diapers*, was published by Seal Press in fall 2005. She is also working on a self-financed documentary film about alternative parenting.

SUSAN ITO is the coeditor of *A Ghost at Heart's Edge: Stories & Poems of Adoption.* Her essays and fiction have appeared in *The Readerville Journal* and the *Bellevue Literary Review.*

SUZANNE KAMATA left South Carolina in 1988 to teach English for a year in Japan and wound up staying. She now lives in Shikoku with her husband and bicultural twins. She is the editor of an anthology, *The Broken Bridge: Fiction from Expatriates in Literary Japan,* and the author of the forthcoming short story collection *River of Dolls.* Her work has been nominated for the Pushcart Prize five times, and she is a two-time winner of the All Nippon Airways Wingspan Fiction Contest. Her essays about being a mom have appeared in *Literary Mama; Brain, Child;* the *Utne Reader; Skirt!* and the *Japan Times.*

KATIE KAPUT is a twenty-two-year-old Irish/Italian–American Midwesterner living in Palo Alto, California, with her partner and her son.

JENNIFER LAUCK is the author of three memoirs: *Blackbird: A Childhood Lost and Found, Still Waters,* and *Show Me the Way: A Memoir in Stories,* a collection of stories about mothering. She lives in Portland, Oregon, and is at work on a fourth memoir about being a mother and walking the spiritual path, and a novel about the Virgin Mary.

CAROLINE LEAVITT is a book columnist for the *Boston Globe* and *Imagine* magazine. The winner of a New York Foundation of the Arts award and a nominee for a National Magazine Award, she's the author of eight novels, including *Girls in Trouble*, a BookSense selection. Her work has appeared in *Parenting*, *Redbook*, *New Woman*, the *Chicago Tribune*, the *Washington Post*, and *Salon*. She lives in Hoboken, New Jersey, with her husband, the writer Jeff Tamarkin, their son Max, and an incredibly cranky tortoise. She can be reached at www.carolineleavitt.com.

JODY MACE is a freelance writer based in Charlotte, North Carolina, where she lives with her husband, Stan, and two children, Kyla and Charlie. In addition to writing, she works as a school librarian. Her work has appeared in many magazines, including *Family Circle*, *FamilyFun*, *Nick Jr.*, the *Christian Science Monitor*, and *Brain, Child*.

JENNIFER MARGULIS has three degrees (a BA from Cornell University, an MA from UC Berkeley, and a PhD from Emory University), but she does not have three sons. She is the editor and a contributor to *Toddler: Real-life Stories of Those Fickle, Irrational, Urgent, Tiny People We Love*, which won the Independent Book Publishers Association Award 2004 in the parenting category. A freelance writer, consultant, and photojournalist, she has published articles in *Ms.*; *Newsday*; *Pregnancy*; *Brain, Child*; *Parenting*; and dozens of other national and local publications. Her weekly column on parenting and life, "Tales from the Crib," appears on Mondays in the *Ashland Daily Tidings*. Her third book, *Why Babies Do That*, will be published in fall 2005. Jennifer lives in Ashland, Oregon, with her husband, two daughters, and one son.

JACQUELYN MITCHARD is the author of the New York Times best-selling novel *The Deep End of the Ocean*, which was chosen as the first book for Oprah Winfrey's Book Club. She has also written four other best-selling novels (*The Most Wanted*, *A Theory of Relativity*, *Twelve Times Blessed*, and *Christmas, Present*), an essay collection (*The Rest of Us: Dispatches from the Mother Ship*), two books of nonfiction (*Mother Less Child: The Love Story of a Family* and *Jane Addams of Hull House*), and two children's books (*Starring Prima!* and *Baby Bat's Lullaby*). Her latest books are the novel *The Breakdown Lane* and a children's book, *Rosalie, My Rosalie: The Tale of a Duckling*. Syndicated through Tribune Media Services, Mitchard writes a column that appears in 128 newspapers nationwide, and she is a contributing editor for *Parenting* magazine. Jacquelyn Mitchard lives near Madison, Wisconsin, with her husband, Christopher Brent, and their six children.

CATHERINE NEWMAN is the author of the award-winning memoir *Waiting for Birdy: A Year of Frantic Tedium, Neurotic Angst, and the Wild Magic of Growing a Family* and of the child-raising journal "Bringing Up Ben & Birdy" on BabyCenter.com. She is a contributing editor for Family-Fun magazine, and her work has been published in numerous magazines and anthologies, including the New York Times best-selling *The Bitch in the House* and *Toddler*. She lives in Massachusetts with her family.

SUSAN O'DOHERTY is a parent, writer, and psychologist. Her work has been featured in *Northwest Review*, *Eureka Literary Magazine*, *Apalachee Review*, and *Style & Sense*, and on Pacifica Radio's *Peacewatch* program. New work has been accepted by *Soundings East*, *Phoebe*, and the forthcoming anthology *Familiar*. Her story "Passing" was recently selected as the New York story for *Ballyhoo Stories'* 50 States project, and her novel, *Brooklyn Heights*, is under consideration by several major publishers.

MARJORIE OSTERHOUT is a freelance writer who lives in Seattle with her husband and miracle boy. She's been writing and editing professionally for over fifteen years, including stints in textbook editing, technical writing, and freelance writing. Her essays and features have appeared in several national magazines. You can read her blog at www.mombrain.com.

JAMIE PEARSON is a writer, mother of two, and American expatriate. Her work has appeared in *Parenting*, the *Utne Reader*, and *Brain, Child*, and in the award-winning anthology *Toddler: Real-life Stories of Those Fickle, Irrational, Urgent, Tiny People We Love*. A native of Northern California, she currently lives with her family in England, where she spends way too much time and money indulging her imprudent passion for first-edition Jane Austen novels. She is also launching the family-friendly travel website travelsavvymom.com.

LISA PEET is a writer, artist, and specialty baker. Her work has appeared in *Mamaphonic: Balancing Motherhood and Other Creative Acts* and *Dorothy Day: With Love for the Poor*, and online at Mamaphonic.com and HipMama .com. She lives in a house on a hill in the North Bronx with her very good and decent son and her handsome little dog.

JODI PICOULT, a New York Times best-selling author, has written twelve novels, including *The Pact, Plain Truth, My Sister's Keeper,* and *Vanishing Acts*. She graduated from Princeton and Harvard and received the 2003 New England Book Award for Fiction. She lives in New Hampshire with her family.

MAURA RHODES has been a senior editor at *Parenting* magazine for eight years. She's also been an editor at *Self, Health,* and *Longevity* magazines, and has written for a number of national publications, including *Redbook, Good Housekeeping, McCall's,* and *Women's Sports and Fitness.* Rhodes is the author of two career guides and the coauthor of celebrity personal trainer Radu Teodorescu's exercise guide, *Simply Fit.* She lives in Montclair, New Jersey, with her husband and four children.

ROCHELLE SHAPIRO'S novel *Miriam the Medium* has been nominated for the Harold U. Ribalow Prize in fiction. She's been published in the *New York Times, Newsweek,* and many literary magazines and anthologies, and she is inordinately fond of her son.

KATE STAPLES was a senior writer for *W* magazine and *Women's Wear Daily* in New York and Paris and is now a freelance writer whose articles have appeared in *Interview,* the *Los Angeles Times,* and *In Style.* She is currently working on a novel. Along with her husband and son, Owen, she divides her time between New York City and the Hudson Valley. Owen is anxiously awaiting the arrival of his sister.

MARION WINIK is a frequent contributor to NPR and is the author of *Above Us Only Sky,* a collection of essays. Her other books of creative nonfiction include *Telling, First Comes Love, The Lunch-Box Chronicles,* and *Rules for the Unruly.* She lives in Glen Rock, Pennsylvania, with her five children, three cats, one puppy, one gecko, and philosopher-husband, Crispin Sartwell.

For more than twenty-five years, Seal Press has published groundbreaking books. By women. For women. Visit our website at www.sealpress.com.

Inconsolable: How I Threw My Mental Health Out with the Diapers by Marrit Ingman. $14.95, 1-58005-140-5. Ingman recounts the painful and difficult moments after the birth of her child with a mix of humor and anguish that reflects the transformative process of becoming a parent.

I Wanna Be Sedated: 30 Writers on Parenting Teenagers edited by Faith Conlon and Gail Hudson. $15.95, 1-58005-127-8. With hilarious and heartfelt essays from writers such as Dave Barry and Barbara Kingsolver, this anthology will reassure any parent of a teenager that they are not alone.

Reckless: The Outrageous Lives of Nine Kick-Ass Women by Gloria Mattioni. $14.95, 1-58005-148-0. The lives of nine women who took unconventional life paths to achieve extraordinary results are documented in this inspiring book.

Beyond One: Growing a Family and Getting a Life by Jennifer Bingham Hull. $14.95, 1-58005-104-9. This wise and humorous book addresses the concerns of parents who are making the leap from one child to two— or more.

The Truth behind the Mommy Wars: Who Decides What Makes a Good Mother? by Miriam Peskowitz. $15.95, 1-58005-129-4. This moving and convincing treatise explores the new-century collision between work and mothering.

Toddler: Real-life Stories of Those Fickle, Irrational, Urgent, Tiny People We Love edited by Jennifer Margulis. $14.95, 1-58005-093-X. These clever, succinct, and poignant tales capture all the hilarity, magic, and chaos of raising the complex little people we call toddlers.